I0152801

Liberating Speech—Today

Liberating Speech—Today

Essays on the Freedom to Speak Out
(or Hold Your Tongue)
in an Interconnected World

RAYMOND KEMP ANDERSON

RESOURCE *Publications* • Eugene, Oregon

LIBERATING SPEECH—TODAY
Essays on the Freedom to Speak Out (or Hold Your Tongue) in an Interconnected World

Copyright © 2015 Raymond Kemp Anderson. All rights reserved. Except
for brief quotations in critical publications or reviews, no part of this book
may be reproduced in any manner without prior written permission from
the publisher. Write: Permissions, Wipf and Stock Publishers, 199 W. 8th
Ave., Suite 3, Eugene, OR 97401.

Resource Publications
An Imprint of Wipf and Stock Publishers
199 W. 8th Ave., Suite 3
Eugene, OR 97401

www.wipfandstock.com

ISBN 13: 978-1-4982-3025-4

Manufactured in the U.S.A.   09/09/2015

Some of the material below appeared in the *Proteus Journal of Ideas*, Issue
on "Freedom of Expression" (14/2, Fall 1997, pp. 3–7) and is incorporated
here with permission.

Contents

1

A Stick in the Beehive
Free Speech in Transcultural Confrontation

THE FUROR THAT WAS evoked in January 2015 first by murderous violence against Danish and French cartoonists who had lampooned Muhammad, and then by the worldwide swarm of reactions that followed, brought to my mind a bit of family lore: Once when my father was a toddler my grandparents found him screaming after he had jabbed a stick into a beehive. They picked more than two hundred stingers from his body, and he nearly died. His very existence (and of course my own, as well) hung in the balance.

No one would question a small boy's right to play with a stick to his heart's content, but that he should stick it in just there could only show his childhood ignorance. Yet, if we should ask what caused the small boy's misadventure, we could have an endless argument: Were the bees the actual cause? Or was it the stick? Was it the child's ignorance of the nature of bees? Was it the parents who had failed to get across to him that lesson? Was it the farmer who had not fenced off his beehives? Was some evil force ordaining it? You could even argue that the mishap was providential, for it immunized my dad to bee venom. Ever after, their stings were mere pin pricks to him, which proved to be a remarkable asset in our beekeeping on a California citrus ranch.

PROBABLE CAUSE AND THE BLAME GAME

I remember a dispute in which a lawyer for the Philip Morris Company declaimed that no one actually had proved that cigarettes *cause* lung cancer. This, of course, was a last-ditch argument. And yet he was right technically; for anyone of a philosophical frame of mind can tell you that it's impossible ever to prove causation from the mere sequence of events. It simply can't be done.

A well-known psychiatrist retorted that the vast weight of epidemiological studies, as well as simple common sense, suggested that cigarettes are implicated. So though absolute proof of causation was, as it always is, quite impossible, the lawyer's ploy to snarl the argument had become specious nonsense.[1]

Causation? What caused the *Charlie Hebdo* uproar?

Cartoonists and others have claimed their recent use of taunt and derision—stick it to Muhammad!—was their sacred right as a form of protected free speech and self-expression. Yet a swarm of events ensued: first, violent reprisals of arson and assassination, then indignant free-speech rejoinders. Many took up the "*je sui Charlie*" chant, and even heads of state met in a show of solidarity. Editors everywhere wrestled with the question whether or not to republish the offending drawings as news, and free speech issues reverberated across the media. In mid-January this furor was met by widespread recriminations and blood-splattered demonstrations across vast areas: West Africa, Algeria, Jordan, Karachi, Lahore, Islamabad, and elsewhere. Copycat attacks have since been attempted as far away as Texas.[2]

---

1. At the moment, the same ploy is being used by British Petroleum to assert that there is no *proof* that their Gulf of Mexico oil spill was the *cause* of the subsequent massive kill of dolphins.

2. Pamela Geller's brazen Texas contest and exhibit of cartoon attacks on Muhammad rather predictably evoked the tragic reaction and death of two more would-be terrorists. Washington Post free speech advocate Kathleen

In this climate, long-smoldering intercultural tensions have flared up and reinforced the soft fascism that has been gaining ground in several lands, as ethnic majorities hunker down against the immigration and growth of minorities.

Some of us can still remember how something analogous ripped the world apart during the 1930s and 1940s; so we become quite queasy. For although today's situations are different, we have seen how ethnic resentments that at first seemed insignificant (such as the racist rant of a few goose-stepping malcontents in far off Bavaria) could infect a whole people, swell into the holocaust murder of six million Jews and a world-engulfing conflagration that killed from fifty to eighty million, and left countless lives upended.

So it is not irrational for us to be wary, though it may be quite illogical to settle into long and fruitless finger-pointing about who or what to blame. For recriminations simply aggravate tensions while proof of causation remains a will-o'-the- wisp. There is a pressing need, however, to review and re-assess many of the concepts, values, and slogans that are being bandied about—the claims to sacred values, rights, and freedoms—especially those we may be in the habit of taking for granted as self-evident.

SYMBOLIC EXPRESSION AS ACTUAL VIOLENCE

One such taken-for-granted claim is that of free speech. We tend to take for granted a natural right to express ourselves aggressively, so long as we do no *actual violence* to others. We seldom stop to consider how culturally relative our sense of *actual violence* is. Many peoples, from the ancient Mesopotamians and Greeks on down, have considered thrusts against personal honor or dignity to be

---

Parker comments, "Not since Westboro Baptist Church's 'God Hates Fags' message and Florida pastor Terry Jones burning the Koran has the principle of free speech been so sullied and abused." (May 10, 2015) That the right to radical dissent is and must be defended as essential to the democratic process does not protect the radical voice from criticism questioning its wisdom."

far more wounding and so more violent, in fact, than mere sword cuts. And that assessment is not limited to the ancient world.

If I wander into the neighborhood of a big city street gang and am stupid enough to *diss* one of its members, I shouldn't be surprised if a knife is bared or even some bullets come my way. Gang reprisals are ugly, illegal and below our contempt, to be sure; but would they be an unforeseeable surprise? Not to the street wise.

A parallel caution applies to our relations with people of other deep-rooted cultures across the world—especially those with tribal memories, prominent in the Middle East. Our own sense of what is *violence* or of what does not *actually wound* is not in force there.

Writing in defense of his free speech ideal, Oxford's Timothy Garton Ash, (who is all for cross-cultural awareness)[3] tells us, "what changes everything is the use of violence to impose your taboos." But, as said, what counts as aggressive *violence* can be vastly different in different societies. For an ancient Greek, an affront to his good name and *arête,* a slur against his honor and virtue, could be more serious than a physical threat to his life. And still today for a large part of the world's population, it remains a greater violation to disrespect or dishonor one's group or person than to strike out in a physical way. Should such a violation evoke a truly violent response, we may feel this to be unwarranted, excessive, and downright evil; but don't we have to look beyond our own frame of reference and our logic, to foresee and acknowledge such a response as a simple cultural fact?[4]

---

3. See Ash's "Freedom And Diversity . . . ," *The New York Review,* November 22, 2012.

4. This is where Timothy Garton Ash, titular head of Oxford's *Free Speech Debate,* seems to stray into a nether-world, with his call to create a common front between like-minded Westerners and then apply what is *logical in their mind,* as if it were a universal, directly transferable to fervent intercultural conflicts, such as those surrounding the *Charlie Hebdo* affair. Writing in *The New York Review* (February 19, 2015), he seems to think we could resolve such issues by closing ranks around our western logic. This strikes me as at best culturally insensitive and unworkable—so impractical, in fact, as to be illogical even by our standards.

Certainly, it was no surprise in 2008 that Salman Rushdie's verbal sallies against Islamic targets in his *Satanic Verses* evoked a life-threatening *fatwa*. And it should be no great surprise today that a large number of Britain's Muslims, while claiming full allegiance to the crown, express understanding and sympathy towards the Kouachi brothers, the assailants of the *Charlie Hebdo* massacre. Those branded as fanatics by one group may remain heroes for another.

CROSS-CULTURAL BORDERS: THE GOLDEN RULE

Today's global media expand our reach far into others' territories, but only someone inexperienced or forgetful of cultural actualities could be surprised when verbal or graphic derision is read as a vicious attack by an entire group and evokes some truly violent response. The real world stretches beyond our own habitual frame of reference. This is especially the case, of course, where people's life-orientation includes belief in an other-worldly dimension to which they ascribe ultimate importance.[5] Their theologies will be impervious to any materialistic cost-benefit analysis and can be swayed only by a more cogent and promising expansion or redirection of their faith commitment. We dare not be theologically tone deaf.[6]

To make these factual observations is in no way to condone or provide an apology for terrorism though it might help us better

5. The BBC reported that while 95 percent of their resident Muslims expressed loyalty to Great Britain, after a couple of months, more than one in four of these still expressed understanding and sympathy for the *Charlie Hebdo* attackers.

6. David Brooks of the *New York Times*, in his *Newshour* commentary, is one of the few who has been realistic about the actual theological interpretations undergirding ISIS members' commitment and the theological scope that must inform any lasting defense against such terrorism. For one of the most realistic analyses of ISIS terror along these lines to date, see Graeme Wood's article, "What Isis Really Wants and How to Stop it," *The Atlantic,* March 2015, 78–94. See also Thomas Friedman's *New York Times* column, "Say It Like It Is," January 20, 2015.

understand some of it. The logic of others' faith may not be our logic. God's ways are not believed to be our ways.

In these days when instant communications inter-penetrate various cultural envelopes across the world, we need to be intelligent regarding the value realities and believed frames of reference that differ from our own and lie beyond our control. In such an interconnected world, we can no longer keep our speech narrowed to the audience of our like-minded group or tribe.[7] What one says may at any moment go viral and spiral out worldwide.

For those capable of imagining their way into very foreign shoes, *golden rule* ethics are universally applicable and, if followed, have real traction. Most of the great traditions quite pragmatically have hit upon some version of the golden rule. Then again, where even a glimmer of the uniquely Christian hope informs us (with belief that God loves even his—and our—enemies), that carries immense, in fact unlimited, cross-cultural force. But even if we don't find ourselves possessed of such belief and are armed only with a modicum of world-scoped street smarts, common sense should warn us that to use derision or person-directed humor carries far more negative force in some cultures than in our own.

As said, that is especially true of tribal peoples who are more corporate-minded and solidaristic than we. Many of us have developed individualistic habits of mind that are forgetful of the holistic and corporate dimensions of our humanity, so we may shrug off a merely verbal or graphic affront to the group in contrast to serious bodily attack.[8] But for a large part of the world, this dif-

7. Henri Roussel, the founder of the satirical magazine that morphed into *Charlie Hebdo,* after an earlier arson had been inflicted on their offices mused, "I think we are ignorant and imbeciles who have taken a pointless risk . . . . For years, decades even, we do provocative things and then, one day, the provocation comes back at us. It didn't need to be done." (Cited by Tariq Ali, February 5. 2015).

8. The recent Hollywood film fantasy playing with the theme of an assassination attempt against a North Korean head of state comes to mind here. It was fated to evoke wider repercussions than Shakespeare's *Macbeth* or *King Lear* ever did in their Elizabethan context. As one comedian commented, if he went to Iran and made such a joke about the sitting president, "that would be my last joke." Most of us recognize that virulent propaganda or religious bigotry

ference is simply not real. In others' apperceptions, such affronts to one's honor may be read as a violence against an entire people. Our speech is free; but we'd better keep track of how trans-cultural actualities here reach far beyond our precious personal right to express ourselves.

Writing in the grand humanist tradition with the freedom ideal comfortably ensconced in the U.S. Constitution, Ruth Marcus felt that other editors should have joined her in republishing *Charlie Hebdo*'s murder-evoking cartoons as news. But she hastened to add that this did not mean they should not also use their own freedom to oppose and criticize such stuff in severe terms:

> There is nothing especially attractive or heroic about giving gratuitous insult, which seems to have been the basic business of *Charlie Hebdo*. The magazine was, and remains, a cross-denominational offender, aiming its juvenile barbs at any and all religions.

Its goal—and it no doubt succeeded—was to transgress and provoke, as with cartoons that showed Muhammad naked.[9]

Free speech and truth-telling advocates should perhaps express in no uncertain terms, *"je ne suis pas Charlie!"* and show some respect at least for the young Muslims who, in their thousands, marched under that banner in Algiers: "I am not Charlie, I am Muhammad!"

CROSS-CULTURAL TRUTH TELLING: HOW LOGICAL CAN WE BE?

Even in our own legal frame of reference, the notion of unlimited individual rights is itself a rather late accretion. Where constitutional law is concerned, no right is unlimited where it may intersect with the common good. For example, where our right to bear

---

masquerading as humor may be ill advised and abusive, smacking more of compulsive licentiousness than real freedom.

9. *Washington Post*, January 18, 2015.

arms, is claimed, even the National Rifle Association has plenty to say about their intelligent and safe use.

In this connection we have to pay special attention to the fact just mentioned, that there can be a tribal solidarity in other cultures or in religious communities that is quite unlike the individualistic self-view that has intruded among us.[10] It is a simple fact that for many groups, what you say or do towards anyone will be perceived as actually having been done to all. This is all the more so, if your expression was directed towards one of their revered leaders or prophets. If it should also be one of those cultures in which justice is conceived in terms of equitable recompense and retribution "to the third and fourth generations," we shouldn't be surprised if signs of disrespect evoke a massive response from the whole group. Here I think is where our diplomatic action, especially in the Middle East, has often been insensitive.

OUR LOGIC VS. CULTURAL ACTUALITY?

If we're going to be rational and logical, even by our own standards, we'll need to be realistic about how perceptions and values that we somehow would judge to be mistaken or prejudicial are nevertheless others' tribal and cultural facts of life, and in that sense are sociological realities of the first order. If we fail to recognize them as such, we will trivialize their actual importance and be blind to the beliefs that have bred them.

For example, if we are Christians who simply react to the Muslims' anti-Trinitarian rhetoric, we may miss the fact that Muhammad's own exposure to Christianity was skewed by his early contact with a heretical Christian sect that actually did think of God in terms of three distinct entities. There is a root

---

10. There are some widely parroted myths about American competitive individualism, such as that it was the genius of Renaissance humanists or that it comes from the self-reliance of the pioneers, whereas history shows belief in a corporate or communal humanity was as strong at our roots—both among humanist thinkers and on the frontier as it had ever been, wherever some were touched by faith.

misunderstanding here that could be bridged by realistic theological discourse.

By the same token, the crucial Jesus doctrine, that God or Allah is not only merciful but positively loves his enemies with the same free grace he commands, is a real point at issue where Muslims and Jews, who do venerate Jesus as a prophet, can be challenged to understand and even perhaps be inspired by his unique gospel. Any coherent bridge here, however, must come from deeper understanding of revelation itself at the core of faith. It is not enough to cobble together some alternative of our own design simply because, as Egypt's President al-Sissi has put it, "*we need to revolutionize our religion.*"

What is neither logical nor rational, however, is to dismiss other peoples' apperceptions as illogical and irrational because we find they do not correspond to our own. We're in for trouble if we discount others' behavior and responses to us as irrational and subhuman and fail to recognize they have their own logic which, because it has importance for them, also has objective importance for the world.

Terrorist actions are hateful, wrong-headed, evil, tragic, and from my perspective totally immoral. How could I want to justify them? I represent a belief tradition in which love even for enemies and prayerful concern for the well-being of all—even for those who deceitfully use us—are paramount. Nevertheless, I cannot logically apply my ethics and values to others' apperception of their situation or to the different value priorities and ethical imperatives that are quite logical in terms of the rationality they will apply. Here I can only observe and listen.

WHEN HUMOR IS A VIOLENT WEAPON

Our reflections on intercultural communication above should make us sensitive to the fact that the actual meaning, use, and potentially violent force of humor, satire, and caricature vary enormously from culture to culture.

I remember a simple scene from student days that brought this home to me. In a Swiss student house, where the tablecloths were not changed every day, someone had spilled a cup of cocoa at a previous meal. An Australian graduate student pointed to the stain in front of a German peer and teased, "Hey Dieter, you've gone and made a mess of yourself again."

Dieter froze, black in the face and balled his fists. Since they had always been friends, he finally blurted out, "Why. . .Why did you say that?"

"Well I don't know, Dieter. Just to be pleasant, I guess."

Clearly, ribbing, *ad personam* humor as a harmless form of entertainment was quite foreign to Dieter. Given his background, he would always look for a cutting edge.

Western performers report a growing popularity for their in-your-face stand-up comedy, along with pop music and videos from the West, among the exceptional young people they meet in the sophisticated night spots of Middle Eastern cities such as Tehran. Though we might suppose that this augurs well as harbinger of a gradual shift towards our way of life and our democratic freedoms (as if the whole world is about to shift into our camp), I fear we would deceive ourselves.

Do we have any inkling of how such incursions of alien attitudes and entertainment may be resented by Middle Easterners? They may be read as an aggression—an actual tangible violence, a culture war that has already evoked more widespread and virulent hatred than we are prepared to acknowledge.

2

Values and Belief
Our Unnatural, Faith-Based Freedoms

THOSE OF US WHO find teasing or roasting humor to play an innocent role as pleasant entertainment, can't be very upset by cartoons that at best strike us as not very funny or in bad taste with their sophomoric in-your-face attempts at satirical humor. But, as I stressed earlier, living as we do in an interconnected world, it is naïve to suppose our expressions, whatever their initial intent, can be corralled and limited to our own cultural group.

Some, feeling that since cultural scorn towards modern western culture is softening in a few urban centers of the Eastern world, believe we should hunker down together, as Oxford's Timothy Ash advises, and make a common universal front for the logic of our position. The problem is, there is nothing universal about our precious "logic," and what we actually may be doing is hardening a quasi-fascistic front in a culture war. As Karl Barth said regarding the last century, at first people begin by defending their taken-for-granted rational ideals, but wind up shooting bullets and dropping real bombs.[1]

---

1. See Raymond Kemp Anderson, *An American Scholar Recalls Karl Barth's Golden Years as Teacher [1958–1964]*, 50.

As a college professor I for years offered an award for any student who could come up with a single human-value claim that is not *belief*-based or does not have some sort of belief system behind it. This, of course, did not refer only to the familiar doctrines of traditional religions, so the hardy freshmen who responded would be dispatched by a few Socratic questions and the prize, of course, could never be claimed. The way in which forthright speech is treasured and hypocrisy decried in our own culture is no exception, but roots into a background of Judeo-Christian beliefs and could not long outlive them.

Columbia University president Lee Bollinger, writing in *The Washington Post*,[2] outlines persuasively the gradual constitutional and social developments that have led to the surprisingly recent emergence of the legal protection of free speech in the United States, but he does so without a word about the indispensable underlying beliefs that have been everywhere at play in fostering the public opinion and political discourse that give rise to legislation.

Instead, one wonders whether he is actually satisfied with an old-style social Darwinist notion, that (given outer socioeconomic development) the unusual commitment to free speech Americans enjoy will evolve almost automatically elsewhere. Although Bollinger recognizes mounting pressures against free speech across the world today, he seems comfortable with what strikes me as a rather sanguine notion that the development of global commerce must gradually lever the rest of humanity in our direction here by virtue of "titanic forces that must ultimately lead to greater and greater openness."

Somehow his word *titanic* sets off alarm bells for me. There are enormous icebergs floating about where entire populations are coming to feel their belief systems are under attack. Where people feel their offspring are being seduced by the moral laxity of foreigners you have an explosive situation. There is nothing automatic about liberating speech.

One wonders if our representative military are not beginning to be regarded as a kind of Darth Vadar presence in places like

2. "How to Free Speech," *Washington Post*, February 15, 2015.

Vietnam, Iraq, and Afghanistan. We've long been treated to photos showing our finest, looking for all the world like aliens—heavy-armored and camo-helmeted—kicking in doors. Meanwhile their controllers sit in the cool blue of distant video screens, targeting drone strikes. It breaks my heart to think that our freedom-fighters across the world may come to be regarded with the same shudder we once felt towards Nazi storm troopers.

Yet that is a real and present danger. It makes me nervous to recall that Adolph Hitler used to speak in exactly the same way about how modern evolutionary forces were working to establish his "natural" principle of racial supremacy.

The burgeoning of forces that speak of nationalistic resentment, countervailing belief structures, and cultural warfare are not to be lightly shrugged off. Thousands of years of war-bedeviled and slavery-burdened history should warn us that there's nothing particularly natural or universal for Homo sapiens here. I'm afraid there's nothing automatic about the values that underlie our traditional commitment to free speech and the kind of grace-founded, love-funded beliefs that stake out its limits and make it work for us.

3

Holding One's Tongue in Freedom
Compassion or Compulsion?

WE HAVE NO REASON to suppose that all newsmen, photographers, and political commentators or cartoonists should, would, or even could look at the issue of free speech from a value-positive Judeo-Christian-Islamic point of view. But those who do, have a substantial dynamic resource to shape and support our rights and freedoms here.

Needless to say, my own faith-based convictions play into what I find to be important. Once at a college party I bantered, "Early morning meetings? Why though I'm a professor of religion, I don't even believe in God before 10:30 a.m."

A colleague shot back, "Aha, but I don't *have to* believe in God at all."

I of course rejoined, "I don't *have to* believe either." Faith isn't proved knowledge. But in what may well be our better moments, we find ourselves hoping and ready to act on the hope we find ourselves given. (We have a distinct term for that condition—*faith*.) Half awake early in the morning another day, as that repartee drifted through my mind, two or three further observations pushed their way into focal consciousness:

1) If there could be a personal God who loves us, the most awesome thing he could do for us would be to make sure we *don't have to* believe that he is there and sovereign over us. It would be perhaps his greatest kindness to leave us free to find our own hearts yearning for the possibility that there may be a creative love behind the universe.

2) If a personal love *could be* at the heart of the universe, the most irrational thing a thinking person could do would be to fail to hope, at least, that it is there and to act accordingly. Pascal used to speak of faith like that, as the sanest kind of thoughtful wager open to everyone.

3) A wise and capable God then, should he have power to shape things to his will, would see to it that he leaves nothing intellectually compelling to force an unwilling relationship. Vis-à-vis God, our intellects are free.

For if *freedom and loyal love* describe God's life, as we are led to believe,[1] wouldn't a kindly God extend his own freedom to his creatures?[2] Here we have the foundational saga of Exodus: Life is grounded in God's dynamic of liberation. If he is there taking care not to pull our strings and turn us into puppets, then this freedom is to be grasped as his greatest kindness. The claim that his ultimate authority and power approaches us only as a suffering servant epitomized that message.

At a high, turning point in the earliest Gospel, Peter blurts out his belief that Jesus represents God's kingly power. But Jesus upends his people's expectations regarding such a power, telling Peter that God's Messiah must suffer in love rather than compel response.[3]

Jesus thereafter keeps tightening this great reversal: "You know that those who are supposed to rule over the Gentiles lord it

1. For the prophets and psalmists, God's *hesed* [or *Chesed*] is resilient, insistent, and stubbornly outgoing (some would even claim unconditional) love.

2. See further in Alexander J. McKelway, *The Freedom of God and Human Freedom*, 11–16, 101 *et plures*.

3. A trans-cultural significance may be implied inasmuch as Mark locates this startling scene in a Hellenistic resort town, Caesarea Philippi (8:29–33).

over them. . . . But it shall not be so among you." In character with your Father in heaven, "love your enemies, do good to those who hate you, bless those who curse you and pray for those who abuse you."[4] Tolerate your enemies: Let them add injury to insult: If anyone should, back-handed, slap you, turn your head and absorb a forehand blow.[5] Wishing your enemies well and praying for them, you will not want to *diss* them. You may "keep silent—knowing that I am God."[6]

TRUTH VS. KINDNESS: HOW JUST IS TYRANNICAL TRUTH?

It is interesting how the first Christian apostles reflect this awareness that a gracious God has not forced himself upon them by any tyrannical power-thrust or compelling, magical intrusion into their ordinary human experience. The earliest Gospel, Mark, makes a persistent theme of how Jesus indirectly suggests his possible Messiahship, yet all the while carefully avoids any overwhelming proof of it. He even avoids any direct truth-telling about it until Chapter 8 where Peter and then others of the disciples have already arrived at this astounding truth claim as a hope-driven belief that is all their own.

Mark pictures Jesus as often tempted by religious leaders and others to make a direct Messianic claim; but he refuses to do so every time until at the very end, during his trial before the High Priest, when his human mortality is unmistakably in view. His sharp *no* to all such temptations is a ground-tone characterizing his life and meaning as Messiah. He takes the way of vulnerable compassion while rejecting that of divinely empowered compulsion. In that way he overturns his people's common notions of

---

4. Mk. 10:42; Lk. 6:27; Matt. 5:43–45.

5. See Matt. 5:39 [=Lk. 6:29] in contrast to a psalmist's prayer, "clobber my enemies on the cheek" (Ps. 3:7).

6. The Old Testament often speaks of remaining still or silent as one's appropriate stance before God. See for example, Ps. 46:10; 37:7; 62:1&5; Prov. 11:12–13; Deut. 27:9; Hab. 2:20; Zep. 1:7.

God's coming rule in favor of something new. The later Synoptic Gospels focus on that by prefacing Jesus' whole career with a keynote story of how, from the beginning, he rejected any temptation to exert overwhelming power over people (Matthew 4 and Luke 4).

There is a related wrinkle to be stressed here: All of the Gospels, in somewhat different ways, banner the fact that it was women who were the first believers and mediators of the claim regarding Jesus' resurrection (as the Christ, whom God will not let pass into oblivion). In the Jewish world, women were accorded the kindness and privilege of not having to testify against others or submit themselves to divulging the whole truth about anyone on trial. So the new truth claim from the mouths of women, while inescapably suggestive, could in no way be mistaken for an attempt to compel with proof .

In other words, the first Christian truth claim was intentionally communicated in a form that emphasizes that you were free of compulsion whenever you began to hope or believe it. (Should you have done so, it must have been because you found it accorded with our own heart's desire.) The all-powerful God who loves you has spoken true: His liberating Word suggests what *may* be believed. But in doing that, he has scrupulously avoided subjecting you to any overwhelm or oppressive compulsion, even by Truth itself. His ways are not our ways.[7] His grace chooses gracious means towards gracious ends.

I would stress again that in the earliest Christian Gospel, Mark shows how Jesus hinted at his healing Messiahship in all kinds of striking ways; but in writing, Mark is careful to point out how all the while bystanders remained un-coerced. Belief was not magically forced on anyone. The message was wonderfully suggestive but never rationally compelling. There was the claim of a liberating spoken truth, "the Word of God"; but this gracious Lord never was impatient in his approach—never mystically invaded and usurped anyone's mind. God is Spirit; but he never simply pipes his spirit into our heads.[8]

7. Isaiah 55:8f.

8. Rather, God is present *with* us and invites us to converse with him "in

Mark had obviously found himself rejoicing in Jesus' gracious Messiahship. But we find he is careful to keep it clear that those still unable to hope so high could and did discount Jesus as demon-possessed. He does not even try to force his readers' assent with impeccably attested eyewitness accounts of Jesus' resurrection, but leaves the claim as heard and reported only by *women*.[9] So Mark wants you to feel your elbow room. Should you as reader not yet find yourself hoping and beginning to believe, you are reminded: You've been left free to wait and find your own mind in response.

Of course someone's bound to suggest that God himself could be behind such studied ambiguity. "Hey, could it be that God values your *free* response?"

It is fundamental then to Christian belief that the God of freedom, who'd rather die than make abject puppets or slaves of his beloved creatures, bends over backwards to leave us free to find and be ourselves in relation to him. In short, he has scrupulously avoided compelling us into his communal relationship by force, ether by the force of reason or by plain brute force. Instead, he has taken infinite pains that we might discover ourselves ready and eager for it—"in spirit and truth"—motivated freely from the bottom of our hearts.

NEWSROOM FREEDOM VS. LICENSE— WHEN FREEDOM OPTS FOR SILENCE?

The *NewsHour* staff of PBS were criticized when they chose not to televise the *Charlie Hebdo* magazine's lampooning cartoons of Muhammad, having judged the material inflammatory. With them I have to ask, even were I called as a news reporter, political analyst, or government leader, wouldn't I still need to consider if my freedom of speech might not sometimes mean, that with eyes wide open and feet grounded on the facts, I will keep my mouth

---

spirit and in truth" (John 4:23).

9. Mk. 16:8.

shut? Doesn't freedom include freedom responsively to hold my tongue?[10]

Isn't true freedom in any arena to be distinguished from compulsive license? In this context, doesn't freedom release me from any compulsion to make public everything I know, and doesn't it empower me to consider a larger audience than my own cultural group and what they find acceptable? True freedom is to be who I find myself to be in direct response to others in community. But person-responsive freedom here is going to express whatever concern I have for other human beings across the world. And that tests my very humanity before God.

So, at a time when outrageous cartooning and brutal retaliations have alienated whole populations and when faced by the instantaneous media's insatiable appetite for new sensation even serious journalists risk addiction to scandal, we might all do well to remind ourselves that our First Amendment right to free speech must include the freedom to remain silent. Won't free ethical reflection sometimes be urging us not to tell all or not to tell at all?

Then again, shouldn't our freedom of speech include not only the right to keep our mouths shut, but the right to speak out to answer someone who has blabbed irresponsibly or unwisely? And should it come to that perhaps, even a positive right to censure and shame the mis-speaker? And yet shouldn't even such a right be hedged about with questions of propriety and simple kindness?

Freedom of speech, no doubt, should presuppose concern that the truth be told with accuracy. But even there, won't we find ourselves assailed by further questions of ethical priority? Sissela Bok, in her memorable book on truth-telling and lying,[11] promotes a word from Dietrich Bonhoeffer:[12]

10. *Responsive action* is actually a better expression than *responsibility* here, since it's a question of ur free converse as we are touched by others.

11. Sissela Bok, *Lying: Moral Choice in Public and Private Life* (New York: Random House, Vintage Books), 1978. See her discussion of the slippery slope of telling lies for an ostensible public welfare in Chapter XII.

12. As theologian, Bonhoeffer gave his life finally for his involvement in a secret plot to assassinate Adolf Hitler , the dictator, who with his barbaric tribal harangue about German racial supremacy, had replaced free speech with

It is only the cynic who claims "to speak the truth" at all
times and in all places to all people in the same way. . . .
In fact, he develops nothing but a lifeless image of the
truth. He dons the halo of the fanatical devotee of "truth"
who can make no allowance for human weaknesses; but
in fact, he is destroying the living truth between people.
He wounds shame, desecrates mystery, breaks confi-
dence, betrays the community in which he lives. (Dietrich Bonhoeffer)[13]

Freedom of speech, as the liberty to lie?

Mark Twain once quipped that George Washington "was
ignorant of one of the commonest accomplishments of youth.
He could not even lie." In all seriousness one has to see this outer
borderline freedom of speech as an unavoidable burden of ethical
maturity as well: for the sake of higher Truth, in extremity to lie.

A Dutch scholar told my ethics classes how law-abiding bur-
ghers of her acquaintance made such a fetish of honesty that they
felt obliged under Gestapo questioning to reveal the "truth" about
Jewish neighbors in hiding. Longtime friends were shot in repri-
sal or burnt in ovens—in sacrifice to the heartless idol of "whole
truth" speech as a right and legal duty.

If I find myself under a regime where freedom of speech is
not protected, then of course my overriding concern as a reporter
may be my own life and freedom to speak at all. Martyrdom, which
means literally bearing witness or testifying to the truth may be
noble, but may not always serve the cause of a higher Truth in
the long run. In these inhuman situations, where true reporting
means prison or worse, responsive freedom may mean biding
one's time to be "wise as serpents," while cooing away "as harmless
as doves."[14] Sometimes, however, as the first great Prophet, Amos,
put it, the Spirit of Truth is "like a lion roaring from Zion" and
cries for expression, no matter what.[15] Here the purity of heart that

---

inflammatory propaganda.

13. *Ibid.*, 154.

14. Matt. 10:16–20.

15. The prophet, Amos, offers an interesting example here: He could

can speak the truth, at any cost, is seen to be the great gift that defines a true prophet.[16]

ETHICAL WAY-MARKERS LIBERATING SPEECH: THE RE-ALIGNMENT OF RIGHTS

One of the most striking developments I have observed during the fifty some years I have devoted to scholarship in Christian ethics and related fields has been the burgeoning on the American scene of two countervailing social values: Vociferous right to privacy claims and, paradoxically, the public's much-championed right to know. These two *rights* often seem to veer in opposite directions: my right to know, vs. your right to privacy. Yet although these rights are of fairly recent vintage, the assumption has taken hold in the popular mind that both are (or should be) protected by the U.S. Constitution and Bill of Rights.

Like Bonhoeffer and for many of the same reasons, I would argue that to be satisfied with the bald questions, "is it true?" and "is it my legal right to say it?" as my sole criteria for publishing or giving voice to anything may sidestep the unique, human drama at play in each of our situations and become a serious ethical cop-out.

Where once the Calvinist claim that even our bodies "are not our own" and should be covenanted to live for each other before a God who has "created . . . all equal," the sense of corporate responsiveness has faded for many. Instead, individualistic achievement and merit have been elevated as popular idols, extolled along with

---

counsel silence: "Therefore he who is prudent will keep silent in such a time, for it is an evil time" (5:13). And yet, as we well know, on occasion he did speak out in the most provocative way possible. (See 1:2; 6:10b and 8:11f.). Donald Shriver cites this text in connection with government collection of citizens' communications in the United States: *On Second Thought,* 21.

16. Consider Søren Kierkegaard's key theme: "Purity of heart is to will one thing." Amos claimed an overwhelming inner conviction as his God-given legitimization to speak out in the King's own sanctuary against social abuse, though he was only a small-town farmer from down South and not a paid official or member of a prophetic guild (Amos 7:14).

the notion that the American way of life should be a cold-blooded, competitive meritocracy.

Since the *Wade vs. Roe* Supreme Court ruling of 1973 inferred a woman's ownership and privacy rights of her own body and fetus, unprecedented claims for private autonomy in all things have mushroomed. This "*right*," never mentioned in the Bill of Rights, has been splashed about as if it were a universal solvent even for such sticky civil issues as marital law, assisted suicide, and abortion.

At the same time, competition for a market share of titillating spectacle has tempted many in the media to disregard privacy and insinuate themselves ever further into personal lives. Where scandal-mongering can bring million-dollar rating hikes, even some serious news gatherers have taken to rationalizing: In a democracy doesn't the public *always* have a right to know? Shouldn't we give the public what they want to hear? (After all, if that makes problems, don't the public have it coming?) Repeat such innocuous-sounding half-truths often enough, and ruthless mouthing-off and intrusion into people's lives take on an aura of respectability.

Sneaking into the bushes, a photographer crawls through his telephoto lens into a celebrity's backyard. Once his poolside exposé has gone viral on the web or been exploited by the London tabloids and the *National Enquirer,* it is gobbled up by serious news organizations. Their cloak of respectability? Since the pictures are of a public figure and have already appeared in the public domain, they are fair game as news. Any breach of privacy or stigma of indecency and personal cruelty lies with someone else.

Such a scenario may sound exaggerated, but it describes an all too frequent sequence of events, such as in the notorious coverage given the British royal family. Syndicated columnist George Will questioned the attitude of some news agencies: When knowing a story to be downright cruel or even untrue, he said, they publish it anyway as an "actual rumor." Should that be news?

There is only one place where we are legally bound "to tell the whole truth." That is in the courtroom, where life or liberty may hang in the balance. Justice demands that such testimony be scrupulously screened as relevant to the crime at hand and hedged around by judicial protections. But even there, despite the safeguards, "whole truth" sometimes damages lives irrevocably in ways that escape the bounds of both justice[17] and human kindness.

Given our media- and information-drenched public arena, we may have become so numb to the way speech is spewed about that we have begun to accept abuses as simply the way of the world today. I happened to be in Scandinavia when the man accused of assassinating Prime Minister Olav Palme was being tried. To my amazement the Swedish media in reporting their trial of the century never referred to the accused by name. Dead earnest about his innocence until proven guilty, they spoke of an accused "forty-three year old male." The court, of course, was open; so if you needed to know, you could find out who he was. But in large, his good name had been protected when, due to the lack of conclusive evidence, he was acquitted.

This felt almost quaint in contrast to the way reputations and privacy can be blown sky high in our American media. (Think back some years ago to how Michael Kennedy's name[18] was trumpeted about[1] or Richard Jewell's in the flawed investigation of Olympic

17. Although this is not the place to discuss it in much depth, we shall have to bear in mind that our definition of *justice* itself here, as everywhere else, depends on our beliefs (or shared belief systems). The American justice system has often taken on a punitive, rather than restorative, face—imposing retaliation and exacting "a tooth for a tooth" payment for a so-called debt to society. But the claim of justice for any action not also embodying true support and concern for the renewal of all (including the offender) is a travesty and is to be questioned by anyone touched by a Judeo-Christian frame of reference. See further my Karl Barth retrospective, *an American Scholar Recalls . . .* , 275–80, 319–32, and 376–80.

18. The widely publicized scandal of Michael's alleged earlier affair with a teenaged baby-sitter evidently caused his brother, Joseph, to withdraw from his 1998 campaign for the governorship of Massachusetts.

Park bombing in July 1996.)[19] Does intense public curiosity justify reckless disregard for good name and privacy? At many levels, we and our media might better exercise our freedom not to speak out so slavishly. Some key questions from the larger fields of ethics and value theory demand our attention below.

LIBERATING LAW

What about the relation between our freedom to be authentically ourselves and the laws that ostensibly defend that freedom? Take, for example, such a broadly recognized law as "thou shalt not kill." Jesus of Nazareth in his Sermon on the Mount points out that you have broken the spirit and purpose of this law whenever you have wished some person away. Dismiss that person as a fool and the substance of your own inner humanity lies shattered, just as surely as if you had broken down and pulled a trigger. Furthermore, if you've been hiding this inner truth from yourself, you have been living the split existence of hypocrisy—itself a personal brokenness of the first order. And your brokenness here wounds the corporate wholeness of us all.

In interpreting Jesus' insight here, those of the widespread Reformed tradition follow John Calvin, who understood this sixth commandment to prohibit not only murder, but also careless damage to any person's well-being, good name, dignity, life supports, etc. But more than that, Calvin taught that this command also mandates positive, whole-hearted active support for all such. We are to uphold the wholeness of others' lives as extensions of our own and in every way affirm them in their freedom to thrive in our company. Our humanity hangs in the balance. Not to be thus-minded is to be murderously inclined.[20]

19. William D. Cohan traces another case of ruthless reporting in the fraudulent Duke University Lacrosse team rape scandal in *The Price of The Power of the Elite . . .* , 2014.

20. For examples of this positive application of the Ten Commandments, see Calvin's *Institutes*, II,viii,13 and context.

When we begin to see God's law in such inward and holistic terms—especially after the entire law has been summed up and defined for us as the "law of love" or "of liberty," or as the "perfect" and "royal law. . . of Christ"[21]—all of us discover ourselves to be complicit in some sort of inner, psychic murder. Who of us has not felt life would be easier if a particular person simply weren't around? Who has not read some obituary with an inner sense of satisfaction? That's psychic murder.

Calvin explained the other commandments and scriptural mandates in the same way, and this kind of up-building positive reading of all scriptural norms became a hallmark of Reformed teaching. God's authority is always liberating authority; so, at root, it is always positive. Who among us has not felt our eye linger on someone we might use somehow to our own advantage? The essence of adultery is not respecting others' commitments.

Psychiatrists have noted how children (not yet practiced in our fine art of self-deception), when they have tragically lost a parent, are apt to remember some angry moment when they wished that parent away. Lacking our tricky psychic defense mechanisms, they know for a fact they were at heart accomplices in that parent's death. So they need help with a very real sense of guilt.

When we fail to acknowledge and confess our inner complicity, or vaunt our façade of moral superiority over the poor soul who finally has snapped and stabbed someone, we simply cinch it: we have been alien to the spirit of this law all along and in the most profound personal sense are breaking the whole-hearted, open community it mandates.[22]

Thus, although the Reformers preached a message of free response and forgiveness, which opened out onto a promised final renewal, they claimed no moral superiority or in-group separation from others. They represented, instead, a hope that is for everybody. If there are hopeful saints, these too know they are but sinners who can light-heartedly acknowledge this solidarity with all others while pointing beyond themselves to a hope that is there for

21. Gospels, James 1:25; 2:8, 12 and more.
22. James 2:10; I Jn. 4:7; 2:21–22.

all. Those who already have discovered such hope remain *simul peccator et iustus,* both sinners and justified, bearers of the promise of renewal and of the challenge that is theirs to share.[23]

JUST SPEECH RE-DEFINED

Something that has not always been so clear is that Judeo-Christian revelation brought with it a paradigm shift in the very meaning and function of *justice.* A kind of natural-law common-sense notion of what is right and just had always impressed itself upon ancient peoples who worked it into codes and systems, such as that of Hammurabi or Roman juris prudence. Justice naturally seemed to require equity or fair exchange. Justice, so conceived, was sanctioned by punitive retaliation and retribution, "an eye for an eye and tooth for a tooth" (the ancient *lex talionis*).

With Jesus Christ came a paradigm shift: "They said to you of old, but I say unto you . . . " He re-defined justice to include human concern in terms of upholding and uplifting all, maximizing their freedom in interdependent community, and, at need, restoring in them its wholeness.[24]

From this perspective if the process of truth-telling and the effect of the media cycle are not ennobling to all (and restorative where offenders are concerned), they are themselves unjust—having become entangled in the toils of whatever evil they are publically reporting. By the same token, the media could and should lead our people in the paradigm shift always needed away from their primitive self-defensive gut feelings about what is just. For true social justice does not consist in the cruel exposure of guilt, punitive retaliation, or the extraction of a so-called debt to society, but in healing.

This is a place where each person has a role to play to bring expressions of forgiveness and reconciliation into every tense situation. As said, if victims of any offense cannot find it in their heart

23. See further in my Karl Barth retrospective, 310–22.

24. Note that the attitude we term "restorative" is here intrinsic to justice itself.

to forgive and be reconciled with the offender, they are caught in the destructive coils of an evil that is in itself just as shattering to our larger community as the original offense. Such a tragedy touches us all, and quibbles about what is the greater evil or who caused it or bears the greatest guilt become quite pointless.

Here we could wish that news people might become committed to lead in the paradigm shift towards the contributory and restorative understanding of justice that each generation needs to rediscover for itself. For sad to say, any news cycle becomes party to the very brokenness it reports if it does not help heal it. Since it remains *human* communication and is not a mechanical thing, it will either encourage, restore, and ennoble our co-humanity or exacerbate the evil. It will either reverberate the discord, or challenge and draw the public towards the restoration of all its members (including the regrettable offender in any crime or scandal).

Some of the brighter moments of our era show that a public indeed can be capable of forgiving and restorative action when the truth-telling cycle has been open-ended in that direction. Think, for example, of the healing experienced by some of those wounded on both sides of the South African apartheid struggle when the Truth and Reconciliation Commission, championed by Bishop Desmond Tutu's group, brought them into conversation. Think of the ripple-ring of compassion that ran through our society, when the media recently reported with awe the forgiveness expressed by parents of children lost in a hate crime.

Again consider how President Bill Clinton was upheld by public opinion that opposed vindictive impeachment over a scandal in his personal life, or how Charles Colson, President Richard Nixon's White House Counsel, was widely accepted as a respected leader with his Prison Fellowship and as author in religious ethics despite his confessed guilt in the Watergate affair.

Leading Reformed teacher Karl Barth used to tease visiting reporters with the challenge that they had the most important job in the world, only possibly, he'd laugh, second to that of those called to teach the Gospel. (And in that role, he often had the newspaper open on his desk.) We could hope that those with a public voice might appreciate how important it could be in their reporting to lead in a paradigm shift regarding the meaning of justice itself. They need to point towards reconciliation and restoration—and not simply expose fault and assign blame. That could give their work a beautiful tone. But as I've been stressing, if we fail to show genuine concern for the offender, that becomes just as corrosive to our corporate humanity as the crimes first reported.[25]

I say this from the standpoint of Christian ethics, but you don't need to be a Christian, Jew, or Muslim to see the long-term practicality of everyone's moving to restore and heal the entire social fabric just as forcefully and rapidly as possible.

A COUNTER-INTUITIVE RE-DEFINITION OF JUSTICE FOR MORE ABUNDANT LIFE

Even the secular civil state can be inspired and drawn towards a concern to heal the life wound that is still agape after an offense has left people alienated. Perhaps someone has been caught in a lie, an ugly truth has been exposed or covered up, a rape has been prosecuted or gone unreported, or a whistle has been blown or forced into silence. In any case, as long as alienation persists, the corporate fabric of humanity remains torn. Peace is equally tattered for all, as long as the ugly finger of blame is still pointing, the inquisition of causation and guilt still at issue, or defensive resentment still festering.

The original crime is compounded and trumped by this new evil in which its angry victims find themselves now ensnarled. Sad to say, they could be even more active in keeping the community broken than the original offender.

Here's an old Christ-told irony: A lack of love and concern for the enemy exposes a crack in our corporate humanity that is

25. See Donald W. Shriver, *An Ethic for Enemies*, 73–74 and context on shared, collective guilt—further, my article, "Corporate Personhood: Societal Definition of the Self in the Western Faith Tradition" in *Becoming Persons*, Vol II, 569–89.

just as serious, in its twists and turns, as the first offense ever was, and even more pernicious since it tends to persist unsanctioned and masked over for some by a hypocritical pretense to moral superiority.

This, then, becomes the larger tragedy and irony of the situation even after a crime has been exposed and its truth made public. As long as a judgmental resentment, a spirit of alienation, or a pretense to self-righteousness persists, the corporate human circle remains shattered for all. Humpty Dumpty has fallen, and the fault lines run just as destructively through the humanity of the *vindicated* victims, of the self-righteous pundits, and of the rest of us—just as deeply (and yes, sinfully, if you will) as they run through the life of the exposed criminals. Some kind of reconciliation must take place—some super-glue (call it redemption if you like)—before the shattered fabric of relationships can be mended.[26]

The irony here can be striking. In the media, for example, investigative reporters in their constant drive to determine and expose legal responsibility often remain insensitive or indifferent to the psychic fact that human beings will not, and quite possibly cannot, continue to live with the rejection and guilt others are dumping on them. If our scarlet letters are not expunged somehow in a true reconciliation, defensiveness and hostility are bound to fester on like carbuncles that may burst into more tragic bloody conflict.

One hears that the one-sided burden of guilt the Allies heaped on Germany at Verdun festered into a key factor that predisposed Germans to identify themselves with Hitler's *Mein Kampf*.[27] That,

---

26. Donald Shriver's books, *An Ethic for Enemies: Forgiveness in Politics* and *Honest Patriots Loving a Country Enough to Remember its Misdeeds* richly illustrate this point. See the latter, 104–125 and especially 110–11; 119 and following: "'Truth' helps reconciliation but it is not enough." See my article on "Corporate Personhood . . . " regarding the societal definition of selfhood that is in view here.

27. Here one must see a real danger in movements that use truth telling about historical evils to lever a present generation to pay for the guilt of their forebears. (One thinks of movement to make Turkey wear the label of past genocide or to make young Germans bear the holocaust guilt.)

of course, is far too simplistic to serve as a historical analysis, but there is something to it where the *Volk* psychology was in play.

I believe that the attitudes current in a secular society may be deeply influenced by those committed to a reconciling message of forgiveness and restoration. Here Jesus of Nazareth's re-definition and recalibration of people's natural sense of justice still carries an incalculable counterintuitive force today. In every situation true justice must include positive, up-building, mutual support and, at need, restoration, or it has not been done. By definition, unresolved rejection and alienation preclude what is right and just.

4

A Freely Responsive Speech
Liberation vs. Willful Compulsion

SOMETIMES IT HAS FELT as if the people of our generation have been tipped into a Humpty Dumpty world. When I was a young person eager to follow a vocation into science, mushroom clouds burst out for the first time on the fringe of our world horizon. In the aftermath of Nagasaki and Hiroshima, we began to see that all the king's horses and all the Oak Ridge scientists weren't going to put things together again. Our hope for lasting reconciliation and peace was not going to be found in physical science itself, nor in all the posturing of politicians and social analysts. Yet the hope of a transcendent justice re-defined and gifted to all remained an evergreen challenge.

So given the needs of the time and despite my personal proclivity for science, I found myself as a young person beginning to speak out as one caught up in the promise of faith; that is, I felt called into the beautiful discipline of theology.

To this day we often feel frustrated, often bewildered, and almost overwhelmed by the shattering tensions between various peoples and interests that bloody each news day. Anyone who has discovered the faith claim regarding counterintuitive, contributory justice and the revolutionary hope it brings will, I think, feel challenged to speak out. For here our free self-expression shares the gift that has come to us as the enduring subject and object of life itself.

IF FREELY RESPONSIVE SPEECH IS GIFTED . . . (ROLE MODELS AND FREE WILL ARE BESIDE THE POINT)

St. Paul's urgent "Be as I am" is often wrongly read as a command to imitate him by doing the same things he did, as if he were urging a pre-set model for life. But if we pay attention to his actual situation and remember what made Paul most notorious among his peers, we see he was saying something quite opposite. As a direct response to God's grace *in Christ*, Paul was claiming for his Hellenistic converts, as for himself, a new spontaneous freedom from external compulsion. This message of freedom had embroiled him in heated controversy with Pharisaic Christians, and he was being hounded by these "Judaizers"—legalists who did not trust direct, individual response to Christ, such as he was preaching.[1] So when Paul encouraged, "be as I am," he could only mean "be freely yourself—in your own direct response to Christ—as I am known to be free in mine."[2] Our free and creative response to Christ is uniquely our own. It does not mean we must ape either him or his apostles.

The Reformed Church tapped back into Paul's drama of authentic free response. This is often missed, since even more than Luther, the Reformed pioneer John Calvin, himself a lawyer, was never shy about urging us to consult and consider all the legal insights and counsel we can—this, as part of a prayerful conversation

1. This is perhaps the dominant concern of Paul's letter to Galatians and is further developed in his epistle to the Romans.

2. For Paul, the meaning even of the old Mosaic Covenant Law, rightly understood, had been to empower the people of the Exodus *liberation* with safeguards for their liberated life. (Having discovered yourself to be embraced by free grace, be yourself; be freely responsive to Christ's insistently liberating love, as I have discovered myself to be. You may be—indeed, are going to be—free like me.)

in community with the gracious Lord, who we may believe is accompanying us all the while.[3] But we may do this in all freedom.

It can scarcely be stressed enough—especially among those of Anglo-American heritage—that freedom here has next to nothing to do with metaphysical speculations about a so-called free will. Freedom from outer and inner compulsions is not the popular, rather mythic notion that at any moment we have an almost divine power to change and determine who we have become and what we actually want as agents. Jesus once said, "Who, by taking thought, can add a cubit to his stature!" That observation is doubly true where our personhood—our inner heart stature as moral decision-makers—is concerned. Vain speculation about free will is simply left aside as beside the point—idle causation talk.

Many, perhaps most, American Protestants seem to have forgotten their Reformation roots in this chatter. For nothing is more common today than dread warnings about how finally we must use our *free will* to do God's will, and thereby determine whether or not we'll accept grace finally—as if we had veto power over God's sovereignty regarding our salvation.[4] Whole quasi-

3. See Calvin's writing "On the Freedom of the Christian," incorporated into his *Institutes of the Christian Religion*, Book III, Section xix, par. 2–14. "Finally faith is imputed to *justice*, which is given by grace and not due us" (Inst. III, xi, 20).

To avoid being tarred with the capital crime of seditious libertinism, Calvin carefully embedded his teachings on Christian freedom within politically correct explications of moral law and pious virtue. But at the heart of his Reformed teaching is the scandalous rediscovery that a Christian's life may become a matter of unbound personal response—from first to last a gift—and, as such, a matter of self-discovery in Christ. See for example, Hundeshagen, *Calvinismus und staatsbürgerliche Freiheit*, as he summarizes, 60–61: "Only that state achieves and defends the noble benefit of freedom whose citizens have the earnest will to become themselves inwardly free. However, no form of government can provide an absolute guarantee of freedom and no constitutional mechanism protects a people from the effects of their own brokenness!"

4. Contrast the pauline perspective of Ephesians 2:8. "For by grace you have been saved through faith, and this [faith] *is not your own doing; it is a gift of God* . . . lest anyone should boast." You don't believe because you decided to push some right button in yourself. Birth is the New Testament metaphor: You didn't get yourself born by having an open mind in the womb or scaring up a decision to accept it. You awoke to it. (See for example, John 3.)

evangelical movements have been given over to this notion of our free will "*Hour of Decision.*" Have we forgotten that the fault line of the Reformation's separation from the medieval Church's accretions ran right through this issue?

Martin Luther with his treatises, such as "On the Freedom of the Christian . . . ,"[5] found this a crucial front against the whole attitude of the Roman Church and its accumulated bag of tricks regarding merit, indulgences, purgatory, and the like. His pointed dispute with Erasmus von Rotterdam just here was fundamental to the Reform.

Freedom to be who I find myself, in God's good grace, to be . . . Freedom from inner compulsions and from outer manipulation or tyrannical ecclesiastical control—that is something quite else from the notion that at any moment I have a lordly power to dispose of who I am and what I have become in the depths of my being. For centuries Eastern thinkers have observed this fact, referring to something similar as the problematic law of karma. Reformation belief is opening in a different direction when it rediscovers Paul's promise that God in grace will finally outflank our inability here, re-create who and what we truly are, and so save us.

Karl Barth used to tell us the free will illusion is a little like that of a beast in a field who feels it is quite free simply because it can choose to chomp away on one bale of hay rather than another, when all the while compulsions can take him by the nose and lead him right away. Without following that theology further at the moment, suffice it to observe that in claiming our constitutionally protected freedoms (freedom of speech, freedom of the press, etc.), we are not speaking of a hermetically sealed, absolute impervious self who careens along with no inner or outer restraint. Does such a mythic demigod even exist?

Revivalism's notion that salvation depends on our ultimate frame of mind, our decision or acceptance, does not co-respond to God's own election (as his sovereign decision to outflank our waywardness and self-destructive compulsions). To speak in New

5. Available in Martin Luther, *Three Treatises* (Philadelphia: Fortress Press), 1970.

Testament symbols, in the strong light of Christ's imperatives, lost sheep cast baleful shadows on his right hand, and ornery goats are darkly silhouetted on his left. But the Gospel takes joy in insisting that no matter however dark our status, the light is there to illumine us.[6]

I wonder what poor sinner's body lies in that Early Christian tomb where some artistic friend, with a chuckle, perhaps, painted the Good Shepherd on the plaster that screens his casket. For the painting shows the savior separating the sheep on his right from the horned goats to his left; but it is an errant goat he is bearing across his shoulders.[7]

The legal systems of different peoples vary widely in their definitions of proscribed speech: defamation, slander, pornography, and fraud. While the law books may tell us how to avoid prosecution and civil damage claims they can make only a blunt approximation regarding what in any given situation might be injurious to someone on the one hand, or what is truly supportive on the other.

As we noted above, since celebrities ostensibly have opted to live in the light of public scrutiny, they can not claim the same legal guarantees of privacy that are due other citizens. But does that mean it is right and good for anyone to say any old thing about one of them as if their notoriety has coated them with Teflon against personal hurt? Loving kindness may well be one the highest, most permanent of human imperatives; but laws can only very loosely proscribe egregious unkindness and can never guarantee or even define actual love.

In this perspective we may want, as a kind of limiting case, to consider public shaming as an effective form of free speech. Can it be a positive deterrent that the rest of us might unleash towards those who only technically keep the letter of the law—such

6. The long-festering debate over "predestination" at this point, I believe, is misplaced, resulting from a misconception of God's relation to Time itself as his creature. See my Karl Barth retrospective on God's simultaneous relation to the times of our lives (130, 288–307 *et al.*).

7. In the Catacomb of Priscilla, Rome, third century or earlier. See Lk. 19:10, "For the Son of Man came to seek and save the lost."

35

as wayward pundits, intrusive paparazzi, or tattletale newsmongers—those who suppose an exposé to be right and good, simply because brutal facts can be lodged in the public record as accurate?

IS IT ALWAYS ALRIGHT TO CLAIM MY RIGHTS?

Another important ethical question is this: Is any human right absolute? In practice our best values often conflict and constantly must be ranked and prioritized. Living situations often set the sanctity claimed for truthful speech and information into conflict with other no-less important rights and values—loyalty to family, for example, or solemnly pledged trust. Think of the evil pressures put on children to inform against their parents under totalitarian regimes or on co-workers to betray each other during the McCarthy era. Grossly evil "truth" telling can be mandated by law, though our law, thank God, does not compel one to testify against oneself.

The real burden of ethics as a reflective discipline often lies just here. Positive values lay claim upon us from all sides, and we must come to terms with the dilemmas: keep quiet or tell all, sacred trust or civil obedience. There's no escaping the sweaty, obstacle-strewn process of weighing and ranking counter-poised *goods*. As limited human beings, we can only rough out our best dynamic compromise and go with it. Then again, "good" principles, so called if they become abstracted from the human concern behind them, can become vicious. So, we've had to ask, is honesty always the best policy?

We've all heard the old chestnut about free speech not including the right to shout "Fire!" in a crowded theater, and such an act can be proscribed (though scarcely prevented) by law. But law can't anticipate what the effective cool speech must be that would evoke a safe and orderly evacuation in every crowded fire situation or even whether sometime such a shout might not be the only life-saving (and in that odd case, necessary) alternative.

Again, we might do well to remind ourselves that right-to-know language can claim nothing like the solid foundation in either constitutional law or ethical tradition that its relatively recent prominence might suggest. It certainly does not fly full blown from the principle of free speech like Athena from the head of Zeus. It should not take a Justice Holmes to tell us that freedom in speech includes freedom for judgment regarding what not to say and who should be told. Unless there is real room to shut up sometimes and graciously disclose absolutely nothing, it is no freedom at all.

Will Rogers once counseled, "Never miss a good chance to shut up." I would like to think that even responsible news people, committed to telling us what we need to know, might still possess their own freedom of judgment here. I am not convinced that it represents an improvement when we're told a Franklin Delano Roosevelt could never become a candidate today, since our present media would feel compelled to parade his lower-limb paralysis for all to see. Is that a liberating freedom?[8]

HUMANIZING RIGHTS AND DUTIES IN FREE RESPONSE

If I clamor under the law always to know—or tell—all, I may be drifting into the most insidious kind of conflict with the very spirit of the First Amendment. Worse, I may be in conflict with our most deeply rooted ethical traditions. Where is the human compassion in lusting to know or tell all? How can it be just to use my knowledge to cut the legs from under someone?

Given our heritage, we are obliged, I think, in this discussion to keep the terms *right to privacy*, *right to know*, and *right* or

---

8. Could many of the great political figures of our past have survived the intrusive media feeding frenzies that are almost taken for granted today? Consider Jefferson, with his mulatto slave companion; Lincoln with his unstable wife and depressive moods; F.D.R. in his wheel chair and frequented by a special lady friend; Eisenhower with his long, more than cordial relationship with his WAC driver; Kennedy with his personal excesses. Some of these things were vaguely known as rumor, but all were left unexposed to the public, as the press of their day exercised an ethical freedom to remain silent.

It should be sobering to reflect on how the threat of shattered family sanctuary makes the prospect of public service odious to many potential leaders today. One need only recall how General Colin Powell expressed such reluctance to become a candidate.

duty to tell all in mental quotes. No subject freely bandied about in recent years turns out to be more thorny under analysis than rights theory. And when rights claims become egotistical or are radicalized into interest group slogans, there is nothing that can collide more precariously with the community values many of us hold sacred.

Here we should remind ourselves that historically neither free speech nor the right to know have been unbounded legal rights. (In fact, neither have any other individual rights been bald absolutes, without ethical limitations or moderating countervailing provisions.) The protection of privacy, for example, goes back less than a century in our legal history. The framers of the U.S. Constitution were of a mind to think much more in terms of the common weal or public good with the individual's good cradled within it. Influential among them were those of the Reformed tradition, who would insist with John Calvin that ownership—even of our bodies and ourselves—should never be forlornly private. "We are not our own" but belong to our Creator for a mutually committed and liberating community.

SPEAKING OUT—A LIVING JUDGMENT CALL

We need to stress then that while legality and truth are immeasurably important, they do not in themselves guarantee real justice anywhere in life. Mechanical accuracy barely takes us to first base where the real issues of free speech and journalistic ethics are concerned. Even if you add to accuracy and legality the further guidance of current cultural mores, as editors usually try to do, the problem of ethical judgment remains.

We may be grateful when a television piece showing a bloody fetus being killed or an offensive cartoon of Muhammad is blocked as offensive to public sensibilities. But if something so superficial as "propriety" is our filter, deeper human concerns may be ignored or silenced in the process. This is what happened during the first years of the AIDS epidemic. The media, inhibited by habitual canons of sexual decorum, were hesitant to be explicit. Thanks to their scruples, the disease got a head start in cities such as San Francisco, and there were a mass of preventable deaths.

The humane *need* to know then should be given a double-edged precedence—sometimes questioning news organizations' legally protected "right" to expose public figures' entire lives, but at other times to override accepted standards of good taste and civility. There are occasions when to shock the public out of its torpor is the overriding thing to do. Real *need* to know can be more trenchant sometimes than either right to know or right to privacy claims here. But no revised rule of thumb can relieve the conscientious editor or discussion partner from having to make difficult judgment calls day by day.

An ethic of free speech, then, requires us to forego the lazy security of fixed or absolute rules. Every public speaker, news person, editor, or potential whistle-blower—even every talkative neighbor is thrown back on her or his own ethical integrity and judgment here. The community's general truth-telling ethos will afford some guidance. But to turn this ethos into an absolute, legalistic rule (that is, to idolize either current usage or traditional canons of propriety) can mean sometimes an ethical dereliction of the first order.

ETHICAL REALISM FOR PRACTICAL DEMOCRACY: LIBERATED SPEECH AND UGLY MAJORITIES

For those who find themselves in a community where the majority have already become aware of the imperfection in themselves by contrast with the love-shaped freedom that will finally pervade a Christ-shaped community, the challenge remains for each person simply to relax and be whole-heartedly oneself in response to all the others. One will experience foretastes of a kindly, mutually forgiving covenant of grace.

Despite our common shortcomings, we may lighten up and remind ourselves that any drive to complete purity in our decision-making would entangle us in a self-deceptive romanticism. For if taken seriously, such a pride-fraught drive would require dissociation from our root identity within community, which is itself very human and imperfect in all its branches, religious, cultural, and civic.

As anyone who has studied the *Federalist Papers* knows, the founders, who toiled to frame a new constitution and then equip it with a bill of rights, were anything but naïve about whether ornery and egotistical human beings like themselves—be they elected leaders, churchmen, or anyone else—would manage truly moral and just behavior.

Nothing could be further from their practical realism than that cockeyed misstatement many of us heard in the third grade: "The majority is always right." It would have been more salient and far closer to their mark to teach us that the majorities in various counterpoised groups will always be somewhat selfish, lopsided, and myopic. So practical compromise between different groups, however democratic, will be imperfect and tentative—never to be ensconced as even a penultimate ideal. For a powerful majority can become an ugly beast and will always be shot through with some wrong.

It was to buffer this fact that the American founders carved out such a convoluted structure for representative democracy, with its electoral college and numerically imbalanced countervailing pluralities—all hedged in at every level of government with structural provisions to protect less powerful minorities and outsiders from the all too fallible ugly majority's power.[9] All this, in a shrewd effort to make democracy safe for the world!

COMMUNITY OF GRACE VS. MERITOCRACY

Our founders could live with such clear-eyed realism about their own human fallibility, I think, because so many of them shared an underlying hope that God's grace embraces human failures all the while and ultimately will heal their brokenness. Such optimism

9. As Reinhold Niebuhr once put it, "the distribution of power in a democracy prevents any group of world savers from grasping after a monopoly of power." (*The Irony of American History*, 11).

could tolerate the earthy comedy of countervailing powers' rough-and-tumble with knowing good humor and political resolve.

As it happened, a majority of them were Protestants (many of these earnest Puritans; that is, Calvinists). So, with few exceptions, even those intellectuals among them who were taking inspiration from Enlightenment philosophy had been steeped in the Reformation's "by grace alone" presuppositions. And those among them who bought into the short-lived movement we call Deism hoped to find a broader foundation common to all rational men for the very beliefs they had absorbed at their mother's knee.[10]

A REFORMATION INSIGT: THE FULL WORTH AND INESCAPABLE SHORTFALL OF ALL

From the Reformation roots, two belief claims were crucial for the new democracy. The first insisted that all people, however fallible and lacking in merit, are to be accorded unlimited inalienable worth. All are, and are to be, unreservedly (and quite undeservedly) valued—fully respected as beneficiaries of God's love and promised re-creation in grace. Permanent, full status is to be assumed and upheld for all—taken on faith as their imperishable gift from birth. People's full membership in community is not conditional upon their merit or on what they, with God's help, could make of themselves, as the medieval church for a time had twisted the message.

---

10. Study those few who tried to distance themselves from such roots (such as, notoriously, Thomas Paine, and to a lesser extent, Benjamin Franklin) and you have to ask whether they were not dreaming to bolster some of the values original to the faith tradition by claiming these had an *all-compelling* basis in our universal rationality—something the Gospels had pointedly avoided.

Some Enlightenment thinkers nursed the Deist notion of a "self-evident" Truth of Nature and "of "Nature's God" that they dreamed would someday sweep away all ambiguity and confessional strife. It did not yet seem to bother them that such intellectual compulsion (even if it could ever emerge, despite nature's ambiguities and people's duplicities) must spell the loss of joyful spontaneity between persons and in their free response to God, in favor of the supposedly inexorable mandates of Nature. In similar vein, the notion of an *all-compelling* dialectic of history did not seem to bother Marxists.

Second, as a correlate belief alongside the founders' sweeping regard for the inalienable worth of all, came their full recognition of human fallibility. In practical, everyday existence no person yet lives up to his or her promised permanent human status. *Nobody does*, whether it is George the Third of England or Hillary the First of Arkansas in question. Since our humanity is a matter of whole-hearted response, all of us experience a fatal brokenness. More or less slaves, more or less free, not one of us is yet the person in Christ we are promised to be: finally "fulfilled and perfect as the Heavenly Father is perfect"[11]—loving even his enemies. The persistent failure to live out root beliefs was most gruesomely evidenced by the way some could rationalize away the evil of subjecting some to slavery or class distinctions, as if Africans or indentured servants were somehow outside of the circle of grace-based community.

Justice was not satisfied by a level playing field where endless competition was going to separate a moral or economically rewarded elite from the dropouts. Rather, Christians' belief-basis for practical democracy required that all be respected as equal, once and for all, no matter what. In this perspective, meritocracy can be as corrosive as plutocracy. Our democracy has been corrupted by too much of both.

Hence in their worship Protestants provided for confession of sin, not just to some religious official, but mutually. In a priesthood of all believers, you are to hear your neighbor's confession, witness to God's full absolution, and embrace him accordingly. This should be expressed regularly as part of the congregation's worship. So the fully restored status of each person is powerfully affirmed and supported again and again by all. No person is to attend worship just for her own sake; each is to be there in truth to reinstate the others.

The contrast between our promised heritage in community and our shortfall in relation to Christ is so pervasive that for us to affect any meaningful ethical hierarchy between each other is both

---

11. Matt. 5:48. The Greek here carries a double meaning, both future-indicative and imperative; that is., "You are to be perfect" and indeed you must be. You are going to be fulfilled and brought to your completion the same way your Heavenly Father fulfills himself. It must be via his grace. His gracious promise is your command, and *must* be. Your humanity hangs in the balance.

a specious untruth and cruel (which means to do so is already, in itself, flagrantly immoral).

If we consider how the belief in equal worth was linked to realism about our common shortfall in the minds of many of the delegates to the American Constitutional Convention, we can better understand their efforts to hammer out a complex and cumbersome set of checks and balances as realistic for practical governance of, by, and for such infinitely valued, but still fallible creatures as *we the people*.

The second belief claim above may sound pessimistic or negative, but since it is ancillary to the first (in which the inalienable worth of every person is axiomatic), it is not to be understood as a put-down or rejection of anyone. In fact, the recognition of general fallibility is a great support for hard-headed political realism, good-humored mutual respect, and functional compromise. With utter frankness, every person's moral inadequacies are taken for granted as a simple fact of life and obstacle to work on and around. For these are believed to be but passing shadows cast in the light of grace. Such shadows make for a good-natured recognition of the way things are. Yet, the all-framing promise of the first claim insures against fatalistic resignation; people feel challenged to work patiently away with playful abandon, and they find more humor to see, accept, and challenge themselves in the light of their gifted eternal promise.

Can Americans still live into the optimistic realism—one could well say, comedy[12]—that was congealed in their founding documents? I don't know, though I find I'm given to hope it.

If all are in the same boat morally, there is not much room left for finger-pointing on the part of the press or anyone else. This kind of realism proves itself to be sane and healthy for workable government.[13] By contrast, of course, it was just such gracious but

12. This, in the technical sense that "all's well that ends well."

13. Notable here, of course, is the familiar system of constitutional checks and balances. See, for example, how the Federalist Papers embrace the practicality of countervailing factions and separation of powers between governmental entities. Also, the disestablished churches would be expected to function as checks against the abuse of governmental power and any pretense

frank coming to terms with all-pervasive human orneriness that was most lacking in the humorless but romantic Marxist dream.[14] Blindness here, regarding our actual human condition could mean eventual shipwreck for communist states—but not before the demonic myth of human perfectability had "legitimized" the liquidation of eight hundred imperfect people a day, on average, across the years of the Soviet experiment.

A LIBERATING PRESS:
OPTIMISTIC REALISM AND POLITICAL LIFE

The above considerations are crucial to the role of a freely responsive press in our system. It needs to be recognized by both political pundits and their audience that if a moral fault disqualified people from public office, then every one of us, truth be told, would be excluded. For in simple fact, we are all permeated with inward moral fault: We do not perfectly love.

Despite that, it is a simple fact that some of us are gifted with leadership or legislative skills. But to pretend a moral superiority over one's political opponents or to pander to that sort of distinction in campaigning or news reporting puts elections and public life on an utterly hypocritical basis. What is to be considered is the candidate's probable ability to function in office, and those people having personal knowledge need to be participants in that judgment call. Even smoke-filled rooms can have their usefulness here. (More so, of course, if free of carcinogens!)

Viewed from our founders' ethical perspective, any tendency in the media to go along with various leaders' or factions' façade of moral superiority is not only bad form, but it is party to an insidious lie and invidious to democratic process. Where the press or supporters' political advertising give weight to the lie, candidates must run for cover behind a façade—*image* we call it—and spend

---

of the rich and powerful to personal or moral superiority. Believed values must be the prime source of legislators' political commitments, but these are protected against any forced establishment.

14. Compare Reinhold Niebuhr, *Moral Man in Immoral Society*, 194.

their energy polishing their image, rather than wrestling with issues. The sad spectacle, when some official's hypocritical pretense to a superior moral or personal status later crumbles, will sour young people on the whole political process.

The question remains: Do the truth-tellers use their freedom well and with good judgment leave candidates enough breathing space to be their human selves—warts, foibles, sins, and all? Or do they wag a moralizing finger and reinforce the growing myth that impeccability is a criterion for solid public service?

If only those candidates are allowed to survive who have cloaked themselves with a fake invulnerability, it favors the very opposite of those qualities needed in government service. At the same time, we lose the gifts of those frankly flawed human beings who could serve well, but are not ready to put themselves through the meat-grinder of destructive gossip or live behind a façade.

We can be bemused by Grover Cleveland's election over James G. Blaine as if it were an old-fashioned fluke. If a candidate today were, like Cleveland, exposed as having fathered an illegitimate child, wouldn't the media cannibalize him? The ground rules have changed, we are told. But could it be his electorate was graced with a practical democratic realism that has been losing ground among us?

Everyone is flawed, and as we've been given to believe, everyone must be redeemed and respected in grace. So ongoing discernment, ethically informed cool intelligence, and humane forbearance are all needed, both by the party leaders who put forward candidates and those who sit in review of public servants. With a cautious, kindly discretion they may hope to recognize which persistent flaws would inhibit a person's practical service and, if need be, good-humoredly spread that record out for public scrutiny.

If the Reformers' matter-of-fact insight into our common condition were taken more to heart, we might be spared some political hullabaloo. But no, we have the media at the ringside, reveling in every low blow to a candidate's image-plexus. Scorecard reporting of candidates' and public servants' personal transgressions can work to everyone's disadvantage, as a mean-spirited attitude of moral superiority diverts attention from their practical capacities for office.

George C. Scott's sensitive film portrayal of General Patton provides food for thought here, showing the irony of how his military genius was wasted during part of the WWII campaign when he was sidelined after news reports that tattled his worst, most unguarded outbursts.

The scandal that stymied Gary Hart as a front-runner for the 1988 Democratic presidential nomination no doubt made public some real personal foibles (including a clumsiness in failing to keep his image façade up and his privacy blinds drawn). But he had a real point in what he later said about the media feeding frenzy that had savaged him:

> We're all going to have to . . . question the system . . . that reduces the press of this nation to hunters and presidential candidates to being hunted, that has reporters in bushes, false and inaccurate stories printed, photographers peeking in our windows, swarms of helicopters hovering over our roof, and my very strong wife close to tears because she can't even get in her own house at night without being harassed.[15]

So you have caught a congressman in impropriety? Facts are facts, sure; but a deeper human concern still has sovereign force: "Let him or her who is without sin cast the first stone" or broadcast the first story. I feel hesitant to mention Jesus' words in the hardball arena of media and politics. But if you think about it, has a tougher, more trenchant touchstone for our present topic ever been uttered?

In a video discussion[16] several of our most prominent TV news anchormen asserted that "the rules of the game have changed," especially since the Gary Hart affair. In the same discussion Lyle Dennison, who was a reporter for the *Baltimore Sun*, de-

15. Fink, Conrad C. *Media Ethics in the Newsroom and Beyond*, 29.

16. Organized by Fred Friendly in his widely distributed video series, "Ethics in America," 1968.

clared himself ready to crawl around in the bushes, eavesdropping or to tell lies if necessary, to get the lowdown on some public official's escapade.

Alan Simpson (then senator from Montana) retorted: "I want to be there with compassion, when you're the guy . . . they're looking for . . . I'd love to see how you'd feel if you were treated [the same way]. You come across as a pretty tough cookie . . . but how do you feel down here [in your gut]—not with your head?"

Should the golden rule still have traction for free speech ethics?

As said, the vetting of candidates behind closed doors has a real place; and party leaders, I think, do well to have curtains drawn as they sift through the kind of semi-private personal factors that might affect a candidate's exercise of office. Sunshine is a good thing, but sometimes it causes skin cancer.

The reformer John Calvin, had a rule of thumb for church affairs that might also be useful here: Only when a scandal has been created in public view should it be aired in public. Otherwise it should be kept privy to the circle involved. To open it promiscuously to public gossip may be more destructive than the original offense, not only to the offender but to others. It is also corrosive to public trust.

Of course, here as everywhere, any rule of thumb meets prudential limits, such as in a case of child molestation. Research tells us that this particular affliction tends to be so tenacious that those obsessed by it often remain a public menace, so communities should be forewarned of their presence. We have seen tragic results when Catholic bishops or Jehovah's Witness elders have kept such knowledge to an inner circle in the well-meaning hope that such offenders might be rehabilitated. This is why mandatory reporting of persons so afflicted, although it may undercut our freedom to keep silent, becomes an overriding prevailing good here for communities' protection. This does not mean that the community will want to turn the sexually warped person into a pariah and withhold support.

To the larger issue, however, an unavoidable question dogs us: Are reckless tale-bearers any less destructive of communal relationships than those caught up in the flagrant truths they blab about? We have seen how the mere fact that any practice has received the aura of legality or popular acceptance or even that it accords with current professional standards, is no guarantee of its ethical integrity. Where free public disclosure is concerned, surely human respect and kindness must be just as important as is a general right to know. When hardball newsmongering—however professional and lucrative—overrides that humanity in order to pander to morbid curiosity, prurient interests, or sadism, it differs little ethically from other forms of prostitution; and since it is broadcast, its effects can be far more widespread, corrosive, and dehumanizing.

If I am a lawyer, priest, counselor, or physician, I probably will experience little conflict here. Confidentiality regarding my clients is a moral imperative kept sacred by professional standards, and I am pledged to speak as legal surrogate for my client's protection against self-incrimination or therapeutically to guard my patient's privacy.

Yet ethical justice looms large on both sides of any equation here, as for example in the case of Roman Catholic bishops or Jehovah's Witness elders who do not have license to keep quiet about child-molesting priests or youth workers. In some states, the legal sanctity of the confessional itself has been challenged in this connection. Should it remain unprotected, by virtue of the constitutional separation of church and state?

Normally, however, a person's freedom not to speak about her intimate matters or testify against herself is legally respected, along with that of those who are in a close therapeutic relationship—physician/counselor to patient, or the lawyer to client. The latter, as advocate, has the role of speaking (or keeping silent) becoming, as it were, a stand-in for a person's own rights in order to speak as one's judicial prosthesis or surrogate—one's *mouthpiece*, as the vernacular has it.

The rub comes if I hold an office in the public trust or am responsible for public media: Is it necessarily presumptuous and undemocratic for me or my small party clique to decide what the voting public should know? The unavoidable difficulty of this question, I believe, should not fuzz the crucial role that still must be reserved for conscientious, sometimes contentious, personal judgment.

TRUTH-TELLERS' ETHICAL DISCERNMENT

That this difficulty will not go away underscores how much we all rely on our public servants for ethical discernment. Our public trust includes our expectation that despite their own flaws, our party leaders and other public servants will show a modicum of integrity as moral agents who, though themselves limited as we all are, will at least try to show personal integrity in vetting candidates. Public hope springs up ever again that our servants will in humility winnow out the needed information here. But as said, their ethical freedom may mean they courageously keep silent at times and not tumble-weed along before our reckless lust to know.

In short, public agents and agencies (the press in particular) are charged to keep weighing possible harm against social needs for disclosure. Free speech and a free press will find their human integrity and meaning as both self-expression and self-control. Here, as in every other borderline situation, where our mix of values can throw us into a dilemma regarding priorities, no one is to be afforded the easy comfort of blanket rules, as if to predetermine appropriate behavior. To tell or not to tell? For the editor or public servant, no less than for every one of us, that tough decision tests one's actual humanity. Public responsibility can shield no one from the ethical arena's final verity: our human heart-response to each other.

5

The Full Reach of Speech
Towards Unity of Word and Deed

"I CAN'T HEAR WHAT you're saying because your actions are drowning it out." Indeed our actions as a form of self-expression are an extension of speech. And below we hint at how that may be having devastating results for us as a people. But then we'll go a bit further to remind ourselves that nevertheless, where faith is present, our hope-charged words actually can speak with far more force than do our actions, which always are lagging behind and equivocal. However, if we believe that the God of grace is accompanying us, always at our side, our responsive behavior begins to show spontaneous expressions of that relationship. Then, oddly enough, our liberated actions gain coherence as extension of prayer[1]—what Paul calls "fruit of the Spirit."[2]

Yet all the while, we exist not only as individual persons, but as part of a corporate entity as well. And where our transnational and trans-cultural relations are concerned, our nation's diplomatic speech is always tested and often drowned out by our economic

1. This relationship was developed in my dissertation on Calvin's ethics, *Love and Order . . . .*

2. Galatians 5.

and military actions. These loudly express what we are saying as a nation and, like it or not, we are all implicated in these corporate forms of speech that represent us.

CORPORATE SPEECH—LOUDER THAN WORDS

Any suggestion that we would presume to manipulate you through economic sanctions or trade restrictions in accord with our own crassly selfish cost-benefit calculations is apt to be read as an unforgettable offense against your integrity and arouse your stubborn hostility. If you, under duress, should actually yield to such pressures, you would probably shudder and begin to despise yourself, and therefore resent us even more.[3]

Recently interviewed by Charlie Rose, the Prime Minister of Iran spoke repeatedly of how the disrespect embodied in economic sanctions destroyed all possibility of his people's cooperation on *anything*. He simply shrugged away Rose's repeated questions about their intended impact as utterly blind to the deep resentment and dogged resistance such pressures evoke in ordinary people. (Even the most self-centered cost-benefit analysis might question whether short-term concessions thus gained could ever outweigh its unfavorable long-term effects.)

OUR LOUDEST CORPORATE SPEECH: MILITARY ACTION

In America we experienced a nationwide groundswell of feeling for the fate of a single boy who was being sent forcibly back to Cuba. But have we failed to comprehend how the death of a single child as the unintended "collateral damage" from one of our drone strikes evokes the bitter resentment of a whole population. They will be united at least here, quite apart from their own factional

---

3. As one may recall, such complexities were not absent from the situation that led up to the Japanese surprise attack of December 7, 1941.

disputes, in their passion for retribution "unto the third and fourth generation"?

How many times have we shot ourselves in the foot by ignoring such cultural realities? Has it been realistic to assume we could advance our national interest by annihilating a few enemies on foreign soil while ignoring the actual hate-evoking effects of our mere intrusion there?—not to mention the widespread revulsion caused whenever one of our unmanned drones (launched by technicians sitting far off in an air-conditioned office) has "accidentally" killed neutral bystanders.

As said, such reactions reverberate through an entire region and are grossly magnified when the populations share a tribal sentiment. A palpable, widely legitimized need for vengeance would have flared up if our drones involved us in only two or three cases of collateral manslaughter. But now we hear our leaders trying to trivialize over three thousand such negligent killings.

COST-BENEFIT QUICKSAND

Americans are often hampered in their understanding of others' reactions by a rather questionable habit of applying materialistic cost-benefit analysis to everything in sight. Too often we fail to see how such a formula is not only foreign to many, but strikes them as venal, insulting, and repugnant—especially where underlying human values are in play, such as personal respect, loyalty, love, family honor, group solidarity, and pride. Such things are not for sale, or at least should not be. For many the benefit side of any equation must show a contribution to humanity at large, and not pander to bald self-interest.

Flat-footed cost-benefit analysis has fed into some of our greatest international policy blunders. Our representatives have not been sufficiently aware that though disrespect and manipulative pressures are not the sticks and stones that break anyone's bones, they are for many much more hurtful.

As said, given their corporate mentality, even where tribal groups may be split by their own internecine tensions, our attempts to buy or lever any of them will be read as disrespect towards them all. Wherever our political and military leaders have ignored or down-played the crucial significance of others' differing cultural values in such ways, their long-lasting resentment should be no surprise.

Such a failure has occasioned what, in my opinion, have been the most misguided international expressions of Obama's Administration, that is, their readiness to sign off on advisors' requests for these unmanned drone strikes into others' territory to kill people they've tagged as terrorists. Our nation's actions here shriek louder than words. They ignore due process and smack of reckless disrespect for bystanders. What American would tolerate similar intrusions into his own land?

It's too bad we can't simply retire those diplomats and military leaders who, on the basis of misplaced cost-benefit analysis, have been rationalizing our national recourse to cold-blooded financial sanctions on the one hand or hapless drone strikes on the other—as if by slapping demeaning or deadly costs on other people, we could compel a lasting peace. Such wrong-headed efforts sow dragon seed instead.

We should be aware of how our self-proclaimed way-of-life-protective actions here have been multiplying our sworn enemies by geometric proportions. Do we still shake our heads in surprise at the growing willingness of passionate young people to strap on explosives and sacrifice their very lives out of a deeply-felt corporate revulsion? When our media brand them all as insanely radical extremists, it can blind us to the real underlying problems. Those who remember how in the 1930s young idealists from many lands went off to Spain to throw their lives into the struggle against fascist tyranny can't help but be dismayed to see something analogous happening in a widespread reaction against what many have come to see as Western infidels' abuse of power.

WHAT OUR ACTIONS ARE SAYING

An ostensibly natural commitment to free speech hasn't kept us from sliding into forms of expression where our actions, speaking louder than words, appear arrogant and coercive—anything but the liberating message we express in our own defense of liberal democracy. What do surgical air strikes out of the blue, with no boots on the ground, say to the people standing around about our respect for them?

Given his lack of military background, President Obama has yielded to advisors eager for him to show himself able to flex his muscles as Commander-in-Chief. They, of course, have argued that surgical drone strikes cost less—leave fewer civilian casualties—than would traditional military action. So we drone on. And sad to say, this becomes our most explosive form of speech. Here, if anywhere, the old adage does hold.

I can hear all your chatter about defense of democratic values, but what have you told me if your drones recklessly kill a single child in my extended family, or even somewhere else in my part of the world? Don't you regard us enough to place the lives of our children above your calculated efforts to influence our political life? Are you so callous that you let technicians sitting in remote offices indict and prosecute opponents of your life-style and, without due process or risk to yourself, murder them and hapless bystanders on our soil?

American leaders' rationalization for such sanitized killing seems blind to the fact that if I were a tribal person, such a ruthless and cowardly-seeming intrusion into my neighborhood would be like poking a stick in my eye. It would evoke the swarming fury and permanent resentment of my entire people. In the ensuing climate, what you call extremism and terrorist enlistments would accelerate by geometric proportions.

We can scarcely imagine the incensed reaction of an entire populace who see this form of warfare as not only ruthless, but arrogant, cowardly, and sub-human. Indeed, it is taken as our most vivid form of speech expressing who we are towards their kind of people. Our actions here will have spoken louder than all the free speech in the world. So what have we won by them? We've killed a few enemies, probably creating martyrs in the process. But we are also winning the enmity of vast tribes and clinching their long-term alliance against us. We can scarcely calculate or even imagine the long-term cost when the heart of an entire people turns against us.

So-called signature drone strikes, then, have been unspeakably counterproductive in terms of our lasting goals across the world.[4] Even our democratic allies have warned of that. Such actions carry our corporate signature—speak for all of us. To assume now that by continuing the same self-defeating, defensive patterns we can do anything but intensify long-lasting enmity is sheer folly. Worldwide conflagrations have flared up from less.

THE WORD THAT TRUMPS ALL OUR ACTIONS

There is one place, however, where that old adage, that actions speak louder is simply not true. It is there where we find our speech to be pointing beyond ourselves, past the foibles we confess in common with all those around. The lovely Word of grace to which we point in freedom and hope illumines and lays bare the inadequacy of our own nascent actions of responsive love. As we are givern to believe, it is the very Light of the World and Giver of All Life who, as he stoops to embrace us, silhouettes, casts into shadow, and leaves behind all that harms or wastes us.

God's claimed grace unshrouds and exposes how our lives are broken and fall short of our highest visions. But this illumination, his liberating speech, and his re-creative action are one. So

4. See for example David Cole "13 Question for John O. Brennan," *The New York Review*, February 21, 2013, and Kenneth Roth "What Rules Should Govern U.S. Drone Attacks?" *Ibid.*, April 4, 2013, 16–18.

in speaking for the One who is infinitely greater than ourselves, we are going to be backed by the Spirit of the universe, who is free to win others' attention and allegiance quite apart from our rocky behavior.

Dynamic faith never would have taken hold and spread in the world if believers' words about God's Word did not point past themselves. Their expressions of hope always carried far beyond their own limited actions—far outweighed the first fruits of grace in their own lives This was true for the original disciples and is just as true for us today.

Those around St. Peter knew his foibles: He couldn't walk on water, ethically speaking, and he too had become disloyal in a pinch. He was limited in every way, as they all confessed themselves to be—in complete solidarity with their neighbors. Yet their Word of hope pointing beyond themselves to One who is infinitely better—more loyal, kind, and loving—had and has a traction of its own and will be heard despite us. Even a small glimmer of such hope shines through any amount of darkness. So the Word of promise in Peter's mouth or ours does speak louder than works. Our deeds always lag behind.[5]

IF GOD'S WORD AND ACTIONS ARE ONE

A complete unity of word and deed is, after all, a divine perfection that witnesses claimed for Jesus Christ, but that we will never meet anywhere else in this world. We do find our actions drawn in that direction by the liberating Word, thank God. But only in his eschatological promise for the radical re-creation of his godless creatures do we find hope for a full alignment of our own lives.

Our actions do begin to open up toward the mutually liberating life we are promised, as we find ourselves responding to his believed loving presence. Until finally, in a very real sense, our actions become an extension of prayer and are drawn toward that unity of Word and action Paul envisioned when he urged us to

5. As the Reformers often put it, believers remain *simul iustus et peccator;* i.e., simultaneously justified and sinner.

"pray without ceasing."[6] This gradual concomitance of all our actions with prayer, as an extension or non-verbal dimension of our speech in a freely conversational response to God's accompanying presence, is a key aspect of the Reformed faith—what we mean by the "sanctification" of a Christian's life, personal fulfillment, or simply living well.[7]

I believe the larger secular society can be leavened by those who project such a nascent faith.

COULD NATIONAL DEFENSE BE ATTUNED TO A LIBERATING WORD?

What American wants to let his people be perceived by the rest of the world as the new Prussian militarists or a reincarnation of Nazi arrogance? Only the *vox populi* of our raised political voices can rein in and guide our nation's projection of armed force.

We could well use our free speech in politics or the media to advance another paradigm shift which should follow from or at least be more attuned to the shift we've described as a needed revision of our concept of justice. This has to do with national defense posture and traditional claims for so-called *just war*. Even the military—its action speaking louder than words—could be expressing a much more contributory and restorative grasp of justice.

History has shown that world-sweeping attitudinal shifts have indeed been possible even towards widely taken-for-granted, ingrained social patterns. Think of the worldwide groundswells of opinion against slavery, child labor, and use of poison gas, for example. The taken-for-granted primary role of military forces could be shifted, too.

President Obama, almost unheralded, laid a groundwork for a wonderful shift here by sending a large military force into West Africa to help defend against the Ebola outbreak. History shows

6. For example, I Thes. 5:17; Eph. 6:18; I Tim. 2:1–8.

7. See further in my *An American Scholar Recalls Karl Barth's Golden Years* . . . 365–66. (This was a key finding of my Calvin dissertation, *Love and Order.*) See my article, "'The 'Principal Practice of Faith' . . . ."

a number of limited precedents for this sort of re-visioning of the military's primary mission to bring it more into accord with our basic affirmation of restorative justice. The U.S. military once assumed such s role in fighting yellow fever in Cuba and the Canal Zone as it has recently in responses to fire, floods, and earthquakes such as in Haiti and Nepal.

The primary role of each nation's military could be re-shaped without sacrificing its peace-defensive function; so its main legitimate role would be seen not as a destructive threat, but as a response force to meet human crises and needs anywhere around the globe. That is to say, the military's basic international mission would be somewhat analogous to the limited role we already assign to our paramilitary Coast Guard.

6

Liberating Speech
Towards Faith-Based Freedom of Expression

VOLTAIRE IS SOMETIMES CREDITED with declaring, "I wholly disapprove of what you say and will defend to the death your right to say it." Although these may not have been his exact words,[1] he was a pioneer of this attitude. "Think for yourselves" he would say, "and let others enjoy the privilege to do so, too."

It seems to be an unavoidable fact, however, that though some world views and belief systems would uphold such freedom, others do not. Liberty itself is belief-based, and a people can actually lose their commitment to it within a generation or two if such bases become unclear. Although it's often ignored, as matter of historical fact, there has been in America a strong link between the Protestant (Pauline/Augustinian) theology and the liberal freedom we hold dear.[2]

The oldest human wisdom known to us, stretching back into Egypt and Mesopotamia, already cautioned how the power

1. See critical note in *The Saturday Review*, June 28, 1947, 36.

2. As I have pointed out elsewhere, this is quite different from the popular notion of free will (or *liberum arbitrium*) as an all-determining human agency. *An American Scholar Recalls . . .* , 118–22; 259–263.

to speak must be reined in by careful self-control. Ancients knew from experience that unbridled, the human tongue can work the most evil destruction imaginable. Like a refrain through wisdom literature as well as in the most ancient law codes we meet the warning: The wise man will bridle his tongue.

ANCIENT WISDOM AND THE FLAPPING TONGUE

A gentle tongue is a tree of life,[3] but a lying, deceitful, perverse, insolent, or slanderous tongue does violence as destructively as the hands that shed blood.[4] The tongue can be a murderous weapon, deeply implicated in sin[5] and as deadly as any arrow or scourge.[6]

So truly liberating speech must be well-controlled speech. Paul in the New Testament was skeptical of those who were making a big deal of psychically released ecstatic speech. Such emotion-drenched sub-linguistic glossolalia is not worth much as communication, he insisted, unless one can clearly explain the love-based freedom that occasioned it.[7]

In general, it is all too easy to use the tongue to deceive,[8] so it became a major concern for Christians to pray that their tongues be kept from evil.[9] The late letter of James was written at a time when some Christians were being tempted towards bloody insurrection.[10] Hence we find here special concern that in all freedom

3. Prov. 15:4; 18:20.

4. Prov. 6:17; 17:20; 26:28; Ps. 15:3 and more.

5. Ps. 39:1; Is. 59:3.

6. Jer. 93; Job 5:21.

7. I Cor. 12:10–13:1; 13:8; 14:5–39.

8. Rom. 3:13.

9. I Peter 3:10.

10. Bo Reicke has pointed out that those visitors to the primitive congregations, described by James as wearing togas and gold rings and politicking small groups, were no doubt members of the senatorial class seeking local support in their effort to regain power from the equestrians who had usurped their power in Rome. Note the surprising reversal of emphasis in James' reminder that after all, the Lord who forbids adultery is also against murder (2:11). The temptation at hand seems to have been political subversion. (We know Early

they bridle their tongues.[11] For though your tongue is a small organ, misused it can spark enormous conflagrations, or like the small rudder on a ship (we might say like the miss-set flap on a jetliner), it can veer the whole community into disaster. So small— yet a superhuman help is needed to tame it![12]

It should be no surprise to find that ridicule or offensive satire was regarded as a violent affront to be avoided. But to have pointed out that speech itself can ignite enormous violence and should be judicious is not to say that speech should never become confrontational. As some insist, freedom of speech can be yeasty in politics only if it *is* irksome to offenders or political opponents.

There is no satire in the world more biting, or more apropos, than Jesus' declamations on the Pharisees' religious hypocrisy. But it was quite clear to Jesus what kind of deathly reaction his words would provoke. The cross was no accident; but it made clear that his suffering servant reversal of Messianic lordship was worth dying for. The fire his speech-in-action ignited swept across the world.

FREE SPEECH AND HYPOCRISY: JESUS LAMPOONS THE PHARISEES

Jesus of Nazareth long ago brought two adjectives for the abuse of free speech into common usage: *hypocritical* and *pharisaic.* The harshest things Jesus ever said were directed against the Pharisees, who were the most prominent and vocal social critics on the Jewish scene.[13]

Jesus' lampoon of the Pharisees was ripe with parody and hyperbole. It had the derisive tone of stand-up comedy or cabaret.

Christians were involved in the assassination of at least one Emperor.)

11. James 1:26.

12. James 3:8.

13. We should be reminded that St. Paul was a reformed Pharisaic Rabbi and that Matthew, who reports on Jesus' speech here, still had contact with Pharisees when he later published, with a grain of malice perhaps, his raw account of how Jesus stuck it to them. See especially Chapter 23.

Some in his audience must have been nudging each other in the ribs: "What's going to pop out of this guy next! How does he have the chutzpah to take on our high and mighty paragons of virtue?" Even though we are two thousand years distant, we can still catch the humor and irony of it. Both Jesus' Daily Show type of popularity and his final rejection by the establishment were generated here.

When he stuck it to the Pharisees like this, he knew he was poking into a wasp nest. So should we think to use him as a role model, we'd better remember that he, as no other, was reputed to be guileless and frank. When he spoke frankly like this, it was with his feet squarely on the ground and eyes wide open, knowing that some would react so virulently as to plot his judicial murder. We also should remember that he also is the one who, according to the Gospels, represented unlimited forgiveness and healing even for those entangled in the very hypocrisy he was lambasting.[14] "Lord forgive them," he is said to have cried even from the cross, for they don't get it—they don't realize the inhumanity of their action. He loved his enemies to the last and prayed for those who reacted with spite. (Thus he embodied the way in which he had recycled God's ancient law, in his famous mountaintop sermon.)[15]

He was the one who counseled us freely to limit how we characterize and accuse ourselves and others: For the attitude in which we categorize will boomerang and clip us. "Judge not that you be not judged."[16]

---

14. The whole of the first Gospel, Mark, is organized to recall Jesus' healing of every sort of brokenness, and he was notorious as having mediated and evoked open, unlimited forgiveness (Matt. 18:22; Mk. 2:7–10; 11:25–26, and more).

15. Matt. 5:21–48.

16. Matt. 7:1. "Judge not; you are not being judged" (Lk. 6:37), etc. It is significant that the Greek word for the judging that Jesus excoriated is related to our words *crisis* and *criticism*, while the word for the accusatory judgment, that he says flat out that he will have no part of, is our word *categorize* and retains the connotation in modern Greek; i.e., Don't presume that I am somehow going to label you. (See Jn. 5:45 and context.)

If all that is so, we'll want to ask why on earth Jesus did not limit his own speech here and keep quiet about the Pharisees?[17] Here is this one, who taught not to judge others or even oneself, lampooning those who were notoriously ready to judge. Here the same one who had told them "Don't think I am going to *categorize* [or accuse] you,"[18] labeling and lambasting this group as a brood of hypocrites. Is Jesus reversing himself here then, judging and attacking these others with the sort of categorizing accusatory truth-telling he has been telling his followers to avoid?

The church found coherence here in its belief that Jesus, as God's own Messiah, is in a unique position to heal with re-creative power all that he judges. He alone could truly meet that criterion for justice. (Otherwise, "Let him, who is without sin, cast the first stone.") It is only if he was without sin, as Christians began to believe, that he is in a position to judge; yet he remains the one who, as such, forgave, healed, and reinstated persons rather than condemn them. So the early Christian creeds envision him in authority "at God's right hand," as our only legitimate and final judge representing the all-forgiving and all-healing Father in Heaven.[19] Whatever he diagnoses and judges as broken, he has already stamped "repaired" in eternal perspective.

17. Some might be tempted to ascribe the harshest of these satirical sayings to Matthew rather than to Jesus himself, for the primitive Jewish church's tension with the Pharisees was ongoing, and they may even have attributed some of the Baptist's virulent warnings to Jesus.

18. John 5:45 and context.

19. "Christ is to judge the living and the dead" (II Tim. 4:1). The one who won't accuse or label, but was known throughout his ministry as all-forgiving healer is your sole judge "The Father judges no one but has given all judgment to the son" (See John 5:16–31, 8:25–30, and more.) Jesus Christ is the one whom Mark had characterized as forgiving and healing every kind of brokenness—mental, physical, social and even a natural storm. It is as such that he is envisioned "at the right hand of God." This messianic image is taken from Psalm 110, but is reshaped now by the memory of Jesus as healer. This vision percolates through the New Testament as the source of boundless reassurance. (See Mk. 14:62; Acts 2:33–36 & 7:55–56; Rom. 8:34; Eph. 1:20; Col. 3:1 Heb. 1:13 & 8:1; I Pet. 3:22.) Note then that where the early creeds confess, "*he shall come to judge,*" this is *not a threat*, but a lofty promise. For this judge diagnoses and heals.

So it is: that the Messiah's whole story has been of unprecedented forgiveness and veiled power committed to healing all comers. It is as such that he is joyfully proclaimed as our *only* final judge. He has embodied God's unlimited power to heal and renew in cosmos-spanning terms[20] His unlimited love remains forever in command. It is none other than *he,* the healer, who shall come to judge the living and the dead.

His followers even went so far as to image him descending into hell itself to bring healing to the worst case offenders.[21] That's a big mouthful! But in accord with all this, they recall him in a unique position—judging and convicting those who were claiming to be themselves in a position to judge. Apparently, the purpose of Jesus' almost ribald truth-telling regarding the Pharisees was to break through their moral façade, not only to expose, but to *heal* the hypocrisy in which they were accusing and bad-mouthing others.

One of Jesus' typical caricatures of the Pharisees comes to us from outside the Bible text. The Gnostic *Gospel of Thomas* alone preserves a saying that almost certainly comes from Jesus himself:[22] The Pharisees are like a bunch of dogs, he said, who go to sleep in the cattle's feeding troughs: They don't eat the grace-given nourishment themselves, yet they prevent the hungry herd from getting it. I take this in context to mean that they are so intent on criticizing that they obscure for all God's gracious purpose (and thus neglect "the weightier matters of the law"). For Jesus the law mandated a liberated and liberating community of persons responding to each other within God's love. The Pharisees' accusatory notion of truth fails to profit from his ground-tone of grace, yet their legalistic growl keeps "the little ones"[23] away from it.

20. Jn. 5:22, 27, 30 and following.

21. See I Peter 3:18–22 and 4:5–6. (This text, as Bo Reicke has critically demonstrated, is quite possibly from one of St. Peter's own early sermons.)

22. Other such sayings are twisted to fit Gnostic speculations; but some are identical with those of the synoptic; so these too, being akin to them, are probably Jesus' own words.

23. Mk. 9:42; Matt. 18:6–14; Lk. 17:2.

This resonates with the re-interpretation of the law we saw in Jesus' Sermon on the Mount: You truth-telling hypocrites, who are so intent on picking the straw speck from somebody else's eye . . . You'd do better to worry about the timber lodged in your own.[24] You're so busy straining out gnats, you swallow whole camels. "Woe to you, *scandal* mongers."

A *scandalon* was the hobbling block that farmers tied onto animals' feet to keep them from running free. Jesus uses it as an image for truth-tellers' legalistic accusations. In the context of his teaching, this would mean these purists have hobbled the ordinary "little people" with legalistic truths that seem to block them from the liberating grace God's whole law is after. God's purpose would have been better served, says Jesus, if such teachings had been dumped on a waste heap or set in cement and tossed into the East River (or its Palestine equivalent)![25]

JUST SPEECH: LEGALITY, LOYALTY, AND MORALITY

We are indeed a nation of law, and no person is above the law. Yet, as we saw earlier, it is patent truth that keeping within the technical bounds of current civil law never exhausts the more crucial question of whether an action is moral, right, and good. At best the law should make us attentive to areas of deep concern. This simple truism from social ethics still comes as a surprise to some: No action is moral simply because it is legal.[26] Laws, being human,

---

24. Matt. 7:46.

25. See text of Mk 9:42–48 and Lk. 17:1–4. One of the most misleading translations in our English versions of the Bible has been here where Greek *scandalizein, scandaloi* have been rendered as "tempting to sin" or "causing to sin." This is quite contrary to the meaning here, where Jesus is talking about those who turn their (perhaps quite truthful) accusations into discouraging *blocks* that trip up others and keep them from a relationship with God in his liberating mercy. Self-important social critics label others as failures before God's law; yet they too fail it outright, and they too need to be redirected by it—light-hearted to breathe deeply the all-forgiving love behind it.

26. See Shriver, *Honest Patriots. . .*, 117 and context.

can be horribly flawed, blunt-edged, and inadequate. They are to be tested again and again in political discussion.

Furthermore, all laws, even scriptural laws, are situation related and time bound. But even more to the point, our most humane legislation, for good reasons, refrains from trying to coerce those inner qualities that most of us hold to be at the motivational heart of what is right and good, such as love, personal respect, loyalty, and kindness. A protected legal right to free speech then does not guarantee that any truth I utter is the right and just thing to say just now in this situation, or that it upholds such prior heart values as these or even the common good.

We saw how libel laws, for example, treat public figures as a special case. Since they presumably have chosen to live lives of higher visibility than the rest of us, we cannot require the usual level of privacy to be their *legal* right. Hence the celebrity's personal privacy may be largely unprotected under the law. But does that make it fair game? Are zoom-lens intrusions to be considered humane, right, or good? A wide body of ethical opinion says, "Absolutely not." Moral rightness is never exhausted by simple legality.

After celebrity-hounding *paparazzi* played into the tragic death of Great Britain's Princess Diana, one photographer pled, "I go right up to the line with what is legal, sure. Well maybe I'll stand on a ladder sometimes; I don't cross over." But does mere legality here or anywhere else in life guarantee an action to be right and good? Far from it—not even when the laws themselves are basically good and up-to-date, having been enacted and kept under review by a democratic process, and are not tyrannical, mean-spirited, oppressive, and evil, as some laws indeed have been.[27]

In a democracy, most of us strive to keep the legislative process abreast of ethical concerns. And for most Americans that means legal authority should serve the compelling public interest to protect freedom and minimize coercion. But knowing that existing laws can fall short, we celebrate the courageous actions of nonviolent civil disobedience dared by leaders such as Thoreau,

27. Consider, for example, pre-Civil War laws that permitted callous mercenaries to hunt down runaway slaves even in New York and other free states.

Gandhi, and Martin Luther King Jr., where they supported the rule of law obliquely through carefully focused conscientious disobedience to particular unjust laws, while demonstratively accepting the onus of prosecution under the law.

The dynamic and often dramatic relationship between ethical imperatives and the politics of legislation is, and should be, a protected process. That this ought to be a civil and graciously peaceful process is deeply rooted in Judeo-Christian ethics and backed by the freely held beliefs of an influential body of Americans who hope their beliefs are responsive to a gracious and liberating God. These beliefs in particular have mandated our civil protection of freedom here—freedom that keeps such life-shaping beliefs themselves beyond state control.

In this perspective, the only legitimate government is a *liberty-defending authority,* and good law must protect people's risky freedom to relate to God and each other in a kaleidoscopic variety of ways (with separation of church and state).

Accordingly, the First Amendment pointedly entrusts our speech and press to the realm of personal drama, and our decision-making here is as fluidly personal as life itself. Control here remains a living question, left to person-responsive trust. If speech is not to be coerced by law, the urgent need for thoughtful, personal judgment presses in. So the legal protection of free speech slaps us with a litmus test of how we use this freedom; and that, as we have argued, always includes the moral option of holding our tongues or speaking out.

WHISTLE-BLOWERS' AUDACITY: A FREEDOM TO BE PROTECTED

Nowhere is the freedom of speech more crucial than when our loyalties are stressed by confrontation with the kind of institutionalized untruth or abuse where justice or redress depends on our breaking ranks to speak out and blow the whistle. Such situations confront our concern for liberated and liberating speech with a special challenge. It will be useful, then, to consider whistle blowing for a moment, for it illustrates in another context an often ignored or forgotten dimension of ethics that we have been considering: What a freely responsive person finds right and good in his particular situation may lead him to break out of his usual norms, or sacrifice some of his values and principles in favor of higher priorities. For what is right and good is never simply a matter of abstract rules or settled principles. Though this is often forgotten, underlying loyalties, diverse goods, and set rules sometimes conflict, and this is as true of our most serious commitments as it is of casual rules of thumb.

Often we find ourselves in situations that confront us with a prior question: Who is your family, friend? Where are the boundaries that encircle those to whom you are committed and owe loyalty and obedience? Are they limited to your corporation? Your sect? Your nation? Your race?

Jesus once asked, what particular good is there in simply loving those who love you. Being a full person means to love even those who don't like you, as your Heavenly Father loves even his enemies.[28]

Indeed his law of love seems to encircle all people as of one family with you with no categories of rank at all. That's simple enough to say. We can easily grasp and perhaps even accept that claim, but no one ever lives up to it. In fact our lives are hedged about with a thousand lines of defense that we enforce with our most sophistic rationalizations: family loyalties, prior commitments, pledges to emperor, security arrangements—on and on.

Edward Snowden, computer programmer for the National Security Agency, who in June 2013 divulged the extent of snooping that was being carried on, has made people more aware that the intelligence services of various powers can keep tabs on the private life of anyone.[29] He warned that the "unregulated" and "uncontrolled" access and ability to eavesdrop and even "watch

28. Matt. 5:44–48.

29. David K. Shipler discusses at length two similar National Security Agency whistleblowers, Thomas Drake and Thomas Tamm, in his book, *Freedom of Speech . . . .*

people's thoughts" represents an "extraordinary intrusion" by technicians who themselves have shown a dangerous "lack of respect for the public." (Whether he showed good judgment in some of the sensitive intelligence material he made public is quite another matter.)

Any whistle-blower must have felt some higher concern or commitment to override his freedom *not* to speak out. And where the public interest is indeed in question, the right and responsibility to speak out should be kept free and protected.

For perhaps more clearly than anywhere else, the issue of moral judgment is bound up with free speech and truth-telling in the case of the whistle-blower. Here, as everywhere else, such judgment roots back into the person's basic beliefs (or disbelief). It cannot be detached from the person's faith orientation or that to which she is committed and believes to be of higher priority than other loyalties. That this relation may be quite blurred in a person's mind or unconsciously absorbed from her ethos, I think, does not alter the fact.

As we already have observed, there is one place that the old adage, "I can't hear what you're saying because your actions speak louder than your words" is simply not true. It is there, where standing alongside all our fellows we point past ourselves to God's grace. Like prospectors who have discovered a seam of gold, we stand pointing, though we're still at one with all those who, like us, are godless in themselves. As said, I believe the larger secular society can be leavened by those who represent and speak freely of such belief.

I also believe there can be—indeed must be today—a cross-fertilization between Judeo-Christian and Muslim believers here. Two deeply committed Muslim students of mine, sisters who both have become religion scholars, volunteered that their father had always taught them, "you must also be a Christian before you can be a Muslim." Of course he had a Koranic take on what Jesus or even Mary had been as a *rasul* or messenger of God and would not mean exactly the same thing such language might connote for us; but there was no gainsaying that a bridge of understanding could grow between us if we would only listen and respect the differing logic of each other's beliefs here.

Muhammad believed Jesus' authentic grasp of truth had been corrupted by followers' polytheistic heresy. (He indeed had personal contact with such Christians.) But even if Christ be viewed simply as a preparatory prophet, some teachings are so central to the memory of Jesus as to withstand such subordination. There's nothing to prevent these from resonating across the cultural divide to become sorely needed bridgeheads for understanding between the peoples of the Book today. One such is Jesus' insistence that God/Allah *loves even his enemies,* and so should you.[30]

A corollary is his enacted message that God, being astoundingly gracious, stoops to serve even the most despised, treacherous, or self-excluding people. God's representative authority, will even kneel to wash their smelly feet.[31] When touched by this vision, Jews, Christians, and Muslims discover a common voice in the world, a liberating speech they are to share.

---

30. There are texts in both Hebrew Wisdom and the Qur'an to the effect that God/Allah *hates his enemies.* Some Christians have hunkered down around that line as well. But this is a crucial place where Jesus as *rasul* would sway our theology with a larger vision of God's love embracing and permanently restoring us all—even though we've been enemies.

31. One of the most significant Catholic ceremonies has been the Pope's custom once a year to kneel and wash the feet of other Church officials—this in memory of how Jesus, wearing a slave's towel, washed and dried the disciples' smelly feet. Pope Francis has been pointedly refocusing this ceremony by taking it to diseased and destitute persons out across Rome.

7

Liberty-Defending Authority
A Zero-Sum Account

FREEDOM OF SPEECH, ALONG with the kind of gracious mutual commitment and liberty-defending authority that must moderate it, has its tap roots for our culture in the ancient Exodus saga and has filtered down to us in various ways through the ensuing faith traditions. Yet as a treasured possession, as in zero-sum accounting, it must be rediscovered from scratch and resuscitated at the level of genuine personal belief by each new generation. There's nothing automatic about it.

It may be useful to think of this freedom as analogous to the larger freedom from slavery. It is only in a slender slice of history—to be dated just a few generations ago with the English evangelical reformer Wilberforce in the 1780s or in the 1860s with Lincoln's Emancipation Proclamation. Although we have begun to assume that bodily freedom for all is a "self-evident" truth, actual world history is as duplicitous here as everywhere else.[1] There is

1. I can't help but don my theologian's hat a moment to underline once more the reflection I mentioned above: What might it suggest about God's concern for our untrammeled spontaneity that, given his sovereign power and infinite wisdom, he takes infinite pains to keep nature everywhere ambiguous as to his ultimate presence and support. Our experience is so duplicitous that

no freedom we can claim as simply automatic and natural for all human beings. Freedoms depend completely on underlying belief aggregates. And indeed, if by slavery we mean the effective possession and control of some by others, we must recognize that there is more *de facto* slavery in the world today than in pre-Civil War times.[2] All Nature—including human nature—is ambiguous through and through. Happily we've been given to believe, however, that being human should mean being and speaking free; but no, there's nothing automatic about it, and each of us begins with a new free response each day.

THE HAZARD OF HAPLESS TRUTH-TELLING

The question bites down: has our penchant for free speech and truth-telling mediated forgiveness and healing within love-founded, grace-funded community? Or has it left people stymied, downcast, and mired in their own inadequacy? The very purpose of life itself hangs in the balance.

Truth-telling freedom as freedom to keep silent is obviously important to the positive role of physicians and counselors—but also that of teachers, artists, playwrights, even of political satirists—coherent with a therapeutic (that is, sustaining or re-creative) purpose. "Let your yes be yes and your no be no; anything

---

we're never overtaken by a univoque experience of ourselves or of surrounding Nature—never directly exposed to an inescapable, tyrannical compelling truth about ultimate things. If there is an all-powerful God, he presumably could suck all uncertainty out of things. But if he is also all-loving and all-wise, would he want to suck the oxygen out of our humanity? Everything would be automatic—There would be no drama left in our relation with him, no place for hope, no gradual discovery of unfolding faith, trust and joy.

Of course this reflection proves nothing. But it does suggest why a God of grace would shrewdly avoid the easy path of proving his presence through a power-grab in human terms.

See the symbolic story of Matt. 4 and Luke 4 on the Messiah's rejection of this mission-framing temptation and the parabolic story of the prince and peasant maiden in Kierkegaard's *Philosophical Fragments*.

2. That is, when we consider the prevalence of human trafficking, sexual exploitation, and forced labor.

else [any added imprecation or prevarication] "is of evil."[3] Those around Christ took him to be the ultimate physician who identified himself with the *paraclete* (the divine advocate, counselor, and aide), the Spirit, whom he promised will be on call always at our side.[4]

Let reporters and hardball political pundits take note. Persons who bring us the news will be tempted to adulterate its content, milk it for sensational scandal and entertainment values, or enlarge their own personalities by intruding themselves to figure within it. Here they are in danger of breaking the public trust in the press's commitment to speak the simple truth.[5] We've had the sad spectacle of how the career of NBC anchorman Brian Williams was jeopardized and the network's credibility hazarded when[6] he was accused of misrepresenting his own wartime experiences in Iraq and elsewhere to make himself an interesting part of the news.

We tend to harbor a natural defensiveness about the particular culture, way of life, or value system with which we are identified, and we allow ourselves to slip into conflict with others who don't share the same values. This is a recurring danger for any group including the Christian church. As often as not, mortal conflict has broken out just here and shattered the human community. It should give us pause that despite all our modern tools for instant communication, such conflicts between peoples turned our era into "the century of mega-death."[7]

History should warn us: If we don't learn from this past, we are fated to repeat its trauma. The older generation in a land like Russia that suffered the full brunt of mechanized warfare would be reluctant to set their national pride or traditional way-of-life above peace. But this imperative is not such a gut feeling in those of a new generation who have not suffered a wrenching war-time experience. The cartoon figure, Beetle Bailey, while manning a canon

3. Matt.5:33–37.

4. John 14:26, 15:26, 16:7 and more.

5. Matt. 5:37.

6. February 2015.

7. Zbigniew Brezinski's term.

says, "I don't get it: Mankind has been at war since the beginning of time. What's wrong with mankind? Why can't we get smart and figure it out?" His buddy hazards to answer: "It's because every thirty years there's a new mankind."

Here is a perennial deadfall: People's natural patriotism and militant pride in their particular way of life tempts them ever again into a defensive, exclusive stance. History should warn us: clinging to their own dear ideal "truth," people often slide into a steel-edged fascism and spawn bloody conflict. Faith-based affirmation of a world-spanning brotherhood of man is like a zero-sum budget. It has to be re-discovered from scratch, hoped anew, and spoken for, by each new generation.

A UNITY OF LIBERATING WORD AND DEED— TOMORROW'S PROMISE, TODAY'S CHALLENGE

And so it is with freedom of communication. Suppression of speech encroaches today as much as ever, or even more. The BBC tells us that China employs some two million people to oversee what is being said on the web and in other media. Russia has clamped down along with a number of smaller states to monitor political expression. Surveillance cameras have become ubiquitous. Meanwhile we've been shocked by how the National Security Agency followed by its German Federal counterpart (the BND) along with large corporations have been squirreling away vast catalogs of our unguarded electronic communication. The liberty of our speech will be challenged again and again. For freedom will always be costly and depend finally on what people are given to believe and hold dear.

Yet behind all this challenge there stands a great "nevertheless." The Christ-told tale of grace insists that a fully and liberating promise may be everywhere in command. We are still inspired freely to believe the bracing promise that all our words of hope and reassurance already have their reality in view, as God's permanent gift. For his Word and Act are a unity. And if that is so, promise is in command and resilient joy may be the ground-tone of our entire self-expression. Let us hope!

Bibliography

Ali, Tariq. "'It Didn't Need to be Done'" *The London Review of Books* (Feb. 5, 2015), 12.

———. "The New World Disorder," *The London Review of Books* (Apr. 9, 2015).

Anderson, Raymond Kemp. *An American Scholar Recalls Karl Barth's Golden Years as Teacher (1958–1964).* Lewiston, New York: Mellen, 2014.

———. "Corporate Personhood: Societal Definition of the Self in the Western Faith Tradition." In *Becoming Persons*, Robert N. Fisher Ed. Oxford, Applied Theology Press, 1995, Vol. II, 569–589.

———. *Karl Barth's Table Talk: Transcripts of Barth's Conversations with His Students . . . 1958–1964.* Lewiston, New York: Mellen, 2013.

———. *Love and Order: The Life-Structuring Dynamics of Grace and Virtue in Calvin's Ethical Thought—An Interpretation* [Basel U. Dissertation]. Chambersburg, PA: Wilson College, 1973.

———. "'The Principal Practice of Faith' How Prayer was Calvin's Key to Living Well." *Christian History Magazine*, Vol. V, No. 4 [Calvin Issue], 20–23, 1986.

Ash, Timothy Garton. "Defying the Assassin's Veto." *New York Review of Books*, LXII, No 3 (Feb. 19, 2015), 4–6. See further the Oxford Free Speech Debate website, freespeechdebate.com.

———. "Freedom And Diversity: A Liberal Program for Living Together." *The New York Review* (Nov. 22, 2012).

Barbour, Ian. *Ethics in an Age of Technology*. [The Gifford Lectures, Vol. 2]. San Francisco: Harper, 1993.

Bok, Sissela. *Lying: Moral Choice in Public and Private Life*. New York: Random House, Vintage Books, 1978.

Calvin, John. *Institution de la Religion Chrétienne*. 4 vols., ed. Jean Cadier, Geneva: Labor et Fides, 1955–58.

Cohan, William D. *The Price of The Power of the Elite and the Corruption of Our Great Universities*. New York: Scribner, 2014.

Bollinger, Lee C. "How to Free Speech." *Washington Post* (Feb. 15, 2015), Section B, 1&4.

Byman, Daniel and Jeremy Shapiro. "On the Value of Social Media: Why We Should Let Terrorists Keep on Tweeting." *The Washington Post* (Oct. 12, 2004), Section B, 3.

Cohan, William D. *The Price of Silence: The Power of the Elite and the Corruption of Our Great Universities.* New York: Scribner, 2014.

Douthat, Ross. "The Blasphemy We Need" and "Blasphemy Revisited," *The New York Times* (Jan. 7 or 9 & 14, 2015).

Federalist Papers. [James Madison, Alexander Hamilton, and John Jay], Isaac Crammnick, Harmondsworth, ed., UK: Penguin, 1987.

Fink, Conrad C. *Media Ethics in the Newsroom and Beyond.* New York: McGraw Hill, 1988.

Friedman, Thomas. "Say It Like It Is." *New York Times* (Jan. 20, 2015).

Hundeshagen, Carl Bernhard. *Calvinismus und staats-bürgerliche Freiheit.* Zollikon-Zürich: Evangelischer Verlag, 1946.

Iacobucci, Edward M. and Stephen J. Toope, eds. *After the Paris Attacks: Responses in Canada, Europe, and Around the Globe.* Toronto: University of Toronto Press, 2015.

Lilla, Mark. "France: Hatred à la Mode." *The New York Review of Books* (March 19, 2015).

Luther, Martin. *Three Treatises from the American Edition of Luther's Works.* Philadelphia: Fortress, 1970.

McKelway, Alexander J. *The Freedom of God and Human Freedom.* Philadelphia: Trinity International, 1990.

Niebuhr, Reinhold. *Moral Man and Immoral Society.* New York: Scribners, 1932.
———. *The Irony of American History.* New York: Scribners, 1932.

Nomani, Asra Q. "Blasphemers Beware." *The Washington Post* (Jan. 18, 2015), Section B, 1&4.

Powers, Kirsten. *The Silencing: How the Left is Killing Free Speech.* Washington D.C.: Regney, 2015.

Roth, Kenneth. "What Rules Should Govern US Drone Attacks?" *The New York Review* (April 4, 2013).

Shipler, David K. *Freedom of Speech: Mightier Than the Sword.* New York: Knopf, 2015.

Shriver, Donald W. *An Ethic for Enemies: Forgiveness in Politics.* Oxford: Oxford University Press, 1995.

———. *Honest Patriots Loving a Country Enough to Remember its Misdeeds.* Oxford: Oxford University Press, 2005.

———. *On Second Thought: Essays Out of My Life.* New York: Seabury, 2010.

Simpson, Alan. in Fred Friendly's video: "Ethics in America." Annenberg/CPB Project, Cynthia McFadden, executive producer. New York: Columbia University, 1989.

Wolterstorff, Nicholas. "Justice and Justification." in *Reformed Theology for the Third Christian Millennium* [Sprunt Lecture, B. A. Gerrish, ed.] Louisville: Westminster John Knox, 2003.

Wood, Graeme. "What ISIS Really Wants and How to Stop it." *The Atlantic* (March 2015).

Index

www.ingramcontent.com/pod-product-compliance
Lightning Source LLC
Chambersburg PA
CBHW071106090426
42737CB00013B/2505

* 9 7 8 1 4 9 8 2 3 0 2 5 4 *